SWORD STUDY

Primary Edition

Written by
Tammy McMahan

Illustrations by
Doug McGuire

Vignettes by
Marti Pieper

Sword Study
Primary Edition

2013 SWORD STUDY, Primary Edition
Copyright © 2013 The Shelby Kennedy Foundation
Published by The Shelby Kennedy Foundation
First printing June 2013

Editor, Jill Morris
Design Manager, Caroline McKenzie
Layout Associate, Hunter McMahan

Dewey Decimal Classification Number: 227

Scripture quotations identified KJV are taken from the King James Version.

Scripture quotations identified NKJV are taken from the New King James Version. Copyright © 1982 by Thomas Nelson, Inc. Used by permission. All rights reserved.

Scripture quotations identified NASB are taken from the The Holy Bible, NEW AMERICAN STANDARD VERSION. Copyright © 1960, 1962, 1968, 1971, 1972, 1973, 1975, 1977, 1995 by The Lockman Foundation. Used by permission. All rights reserved.

Scripture quotations identified NIV are taken from the HOLY BIBLE, NEW INTERNATIONAL VERSION. Copyright © 1973, 1978, 1984 by the International Bible Society. Used by permission of International Bible Society. All rights reserved.

Scripture quotations identified ESV are taken from The English Standard Version. Copyright © 1993, 1994, 1995, 1996, 2000, 2001, 2002. Used by permission, Crossway Division of Good News Publishers. All rights reserved.

Word Study Part A entries based on Strong's Exhaustive Concordance of the Bible and Greek Dictionary of the New Testament. Word Study Part B entries are based on Vine's Concise Dictionary of the Bible Zodhiates' Complete Word Study: New Testament.

Printed in the United States of America.

For more information about resources for studying the Bible together as a family, or to order additional copies of this resource, visit www.biblebee.org.

DEDICATION

*To the glory and honor of Jesus
Christ, Son of the living God.*

*To Abigail, my youngest Timothy:
keep your eyes fixed on Jesus, walk
in His light and continue to seek Him
diligently!*

4

SECTIONS

WEEK AT GLANCE

Weekly

AN INTRODUCTORY STORY

The first day of each week will begin with a vignette. It is designed to be a prelude to the main themes that you will be studying during the week.

FIVE DAYS OF STUDY

You will be led through five days of study each week. Each book's chapter will be studied over a two-week period, starting with an overview of the chapter and then moving through the Investigative Study to a final "Day 10 Diagram" summary of the entire chapter at the end of the two-week period.

Daily

ON YOUR KNEES: PRAY, WRITE, READ

You will begin each day by praying for a quiet and focused heart. Then, you will write out verses to create your own copy of Scripture in the WRITE! tab and read through the book.

INVESTIGATIVE STUDY: 1-2-3

You will be led through simple steps in your Investigative Study by allowing Scripture to interpret Scripture.

APPLY!

Each week, you will apply what you have learned through practical activities.

Continued on next page...

WEEK AT GLANCE

Daily	

A.C.T.S. Prayer

Each day will conclude with a guided prayer time to help you think through the Scriptures you investigated in your study. Initially, we will pray through each step of the A.C.T.S. prayer model. After the first week, we encourage you to write personal prayers within the Sword Study .

A - Adoration

In Adoration we will worship God for who He is and what He has done. We will focus on His character, attributes, and/or deeds that we saw in His Word that day.

C - Confession

In our time of Confession we will focus on our sin. We will take God's Word, hold it up to our hearts and our lives to see where we miss the mark. You will be led to go before the Lord and confess.

T - Thanksgiving

As we go to the Lord in Thanksgiving, we will express our gratitude to God for who He is and what He has done. We will thank Him for what we have learned about Him that day and for what He has revealed to us in His Word.

S - Supplication

When we approach God in Supplication, we will bring those study-related prayer requests before His throne. Instead of focusing on our circumstances, we will focus on what we have learned in His Word that day and ask Him to help us apply those truths to our lives.

Sword Study Overview
Investigative Study: 1-2-3 Apply!

1 - The Aerial View

From our knees, we will move into our INVESTIGATIVE STUDY of the Bible. Your study begins with the AERIAL VIEW, in which you will read the entire book several times to help you become familiar with the text. This will show you the "lay of the land," like a photo taken from an airplane or a satellite. By researching the author, historical context and original recipients of the book, you will set the stage for more accurate understanding of the text. You will create your own book title that describes the central theme of the book. Your AERIAL VIEW observations will help you build a solid and true foundation for all that you will learn in the upcoming weeks. The AERIAL VIEW will be covered in Week One as we investigate the author, recipient, and the historical context of the book.

2 - The Streetview

As we continue, we will explore the book from a STREETVIEW perspective, going in for a closer look and focusing in on one chapter at a time. The STREETVIEW involves several exercises. First, you will make general observations of the chapter by looking for exhortations, commands, topics, or lists. Then, you will literally be interviewing the chapter by asking who, what, when, where, why, and how questions. This exercise will be like knocking on someone's door and asking them questions. Next, you will search the chapter for any Key Words. Finally, from these observations, you will choose a title for the chapter. In addition, as part of the daily INVESTIGATIVE STUDY, you will read through the chapter being studied, making any new or revised observations of the chapter.

3 - Under the Rug

UNDER THE RUG is when we really dig deep to uncover any hidden details. In this step, we will be identifying specific Key Words and looking up the original Greek words and their meanings. We refer to this step as a "Word Study." We will also look up cross references for the key words. These are Scriptures in other parts of the Bible that will provide deeper understanding and context for the Key Word.

Apply!

APPLY! is where we put it all together – from all the different views – to find what God reveals to us through our study of His Word. This will happen at different levels, depending on where you are in the chapter and on what part of the INVESTIGATIVE STUDY process you are in. Until you finish the UNDER THE RUG level, the APPLY! step will pertain in a general way to what you studied weekly. Then on the last day of each chapter, you will have an opportunity to summarize through the unique "Day 10 Diagram". Finally, you will be able to apply what you have studied to how you live.

STUDY OF 1 JOHN
A 12-Week Discipleship Study

Written by
Tammy McMahan

Illustrations by
Doug McGuire

Vignettes by
Marti Pieper

CONTENTS

FOCUS SCRIPTURES

"Thus says the LORD, 'Let not a wise man boast of his wisdom, and let not the mighty man boast of his might, let not a rich man boast of his riches; but let him who boasts boast of this, that he understands and knows Me, that I am the LORD who exercises lovingkindness, justice and righteousness on earth; for I delight in these things,' declares the LORD."

Jeremiah 9:23-24
New American Standard Bible

"These things have I written unto you that believe on the name of the Son of God; that ye may know that ye have eternal life, and that ye may believe on the name of the Son of God."

1 John 5:13
King James Version

The Visitor

"Mmmmm, I love making cookies!" Melanie said as she watched her older sister stir the butter and brown sugar together in the bright blue mixing bowl.

"Don't you mean you love eating them?" Andrew chimed in as he looked up from his algebra. "Karissa's doing all the work."

"I love eating them best," Melanie grinned. "But making them is fun, too."

"Is that so?" Karissa smiled as she passed the bowl to her sister. "How about if you take a turn?"

"Thanks for working together, you two," Mom said as she entered the room with a loaded laundry basket in her arms. "We need the cookies wrapped and ready by 2:00."

"2:00?" Andrew paused again. "What's so special about 2:00?"

"Don't you remember? The UPS man always comes after that time," Karissa reminded her brother. "We're making a plate of cookies just for him."

"That's right," Melanie added. "The Bible Bee boxes went out two days ago, and Dad says they'll be here today. I can't wait to get our new Sword Studies!"

"Oh, I get it!" Andrew nodded. "Cookies make a great way to say 'thanks' to the UPS man. Say, I could use a little thank-you message, too!"

"I don't know why we're thanking you, but I'm sure you'll get plenty of cookies," Karissa said, dropping spoonfuls of dough onto the pan.

"For being the best big brother ever, of course!"

"Best—and only," Melanie commented. "But hurry, we need to get this pan in the oven! And Andrew, after you win that $100,000 top Senior Division prize at Bible Bee Nationals, you can buy all the cookies you want."

"For sure!" Karissa said. "You can even pay us to make them. But since we're going to win, too, we may not need the money."

"Wait a minute," a deep voice interrupted the friendly discussion. There in the kitchen stood a bearded, white-haired man dressed in a rough robe and sandals. "Aren't you three forgetting something?"

"Wait—what?" Andrew was the first to stutter out a response. "Who are you? *What* are you?"

"I'm the apostle John, author of the book you'll study for the next twelve weeks."

"Yeah, right," Melanie said, suspicion bathing her voice. "Dad? Are you trying to trick us again?"

Karissa stared, silent. One hand held a spoonful of cookie dough suspended over the pan.

"You may not believe this, but I really am the apostle John," the visitor continued. "They don't let me visit very often. But I thought you might need a dose of encouragement."

"Dose of encouragement?" said Melanie. "How about 'dose of sheer terror'? Did we go to sleep and wake up in *Adventures in Odyssey?*"

"Not at all," John reassured her. "Your guardian angels and I just wanted to assure you of the importance of what you are going to learn this summer. I can only stay a few minutes, but believe me, there's a lot more to the Bible Bee than the cash awards. May I tell you about this year's Sword Study?"

"Go ahead," said Karissa, slipping the pan of cookies into the oven.

John's brown eyes shone with excitement. "First of all, do you know what book we'll cover this year?"

"Our boxes haven't come yet, so no, we don't know," answered Melanie.

"All the more reason for me to tell you about my book."

"Your book? We must be studying the Gospel of John!"

"Not so fast, little sister," John cautioned. "I wrote more than one New Testament book. You remember that, don't you?"

Karissa nodded. "I know I do! You wrote the Gospel of John, but you also wrote the last book of the New Testament: Revelation."

"And let's not forget the others," added Andrew. "1 John, 2 John and 3 John. They're tiny, but mighty."

"Exactly!" John smiled at his new friends. "You've got it. Our focal book is the little one you call '1 John.' It's one of my favorites."

"1 John!" exclaimed Andrew. "Nothing to it!"

"Oh, you might be surprised," the apostle responded. "Like any good author, I know how to pack plenty of truth in a few words."

"But isn't 1 John like, umm, a letter or something?" asked Melanie. "No wonder it's so short."

You're right," John said. "This book isn't very long. It only has five little chapters, but holds essential truths that are far more valuable than any monetary prize. As you investigate each chapter deeply through your Sword Studies, you'll learn how you can know and follow God better in your lives today, though initially, I wrote it for my friends."

"Your friends?" Karissa asked. "Like some of the other apostles?"

"Not quite," John responded. "In this case, the 'friend' was a church—actually, several churches. I wrote the letter as a warning."

"A warning?" Andrew wrinkled his forehead.

"I wanted to warn my friends. We didn't have the Internet, but we still had lots of false teaching. Some people were saying Jesus wasn't God!" John sighed. "I wrote my book so my friends could know the truth."

"Know the truth," Melanie said. "Mom's always saying that. And here she comes!"

In that instant, John disappeared. "Do you have the cookies done?" Mom asked, opening the door leading from the basement. "I can hardly wait for those boxes to arrive. And I love the way the Sword Study lets us all study the same thing at the same time."

"I do, too!" Melanie answered. "I bet the apostle John has all kinds of things to teach us!"

"The apostle John—but how . . . did the UPS driver already come?"

"Not yet. But you know me. I just want to know the truth." Melanie paused with a knowing look at her siblings. "And this time, I have a feeling it'll come through the apostle John. Hurry! I think I hear the delivery truck now!"

(to be continued)

DAY ONE

ON MY KNEES:

Greetings, young explorer! You are going to really like the book of 1 John! The whole Bible is filled with treasure hunts to learn more about God. He loves you more than you can imagine. In this study of 1 John, you will find many great treasures. Learning how to have a real friendship with God is the best one!

First, you should find a good spot to do your Bible study. The perfect place would be quiet and bright. Your location should include a table big enough to spread out your Bible and Sword Study. Finally, you will want to have a sharpened pencil and colored pencils.

Now, let's talk about the pattern of your Sword Study. Every day you will begin with an ON YOUR KNEES section. Here you will pray, write verses and read from the book of 1 John. Since today is your first day, we will explain each section as we go. We always start with prayer. We will give you ideas, but you can pray what you would like.

PRAY

"Dear Jesus, I am all ready to study Your Word. Help me focus without interruption. Give me the strength to stick with this study of 1 John. In Your Son Jesus' name I pray. Amen."

WRITE

We are going to write verses that encourage us to spend time with the Lord. Turn to Psalm 145:18 and write the verse on the lines below.

_____

_____

_____

_____

_____

READ

Each day you will read one chapter of 1 John before you begin the INVESTI-GATIVE STUDY section of your Sword Study. **WAIT**...this week is different. On Days One and Five we want you to read the whole letter of 1 John. You may read some words you don't know, just circle them as you go. Open up your Bible and read all of 1 John. This may sound hard, but YOU CAN DO IT!

INVESTIGATIVE STUDY
AERIAL VIEW: THE BIG PICTURE

The INVESTIGATIVE STUDY section is next. You have done a lot of work already, so we will just answer a few overview questions about 1 John.

Is 1 John in the Old Testament or the New Testament?

_____

Was this letter written before or after Jesus was born? (Hint: 1 John 5:20)

_____

Were there any words that you circled as you read 1 John? Write them on the line below.

_____

Apply!

"Iron sharpens iron, and one man sharpens another." Proverbs 27:17 ESV

Every once in a while you will have an "Apply" section. Here we will give you an activity to live out what you have learned in your study. The verse above tells us that iron sharpens iron. Having someone to encourage you to study God's Word will help keep you going when it gets hard.

Call or write to one of your grandparents or another older person that is close to you and tell him or her that you started a Bible study on 1 John. Ask him or her to give you "check-up" calls to see how your study is going over the coming weeks.

A.C.T.S. Prayer Time

Before we finish our time with God in His Word, it is good to end by praying. Again, we will give you some short prayers to give you a starting point; often we will use a verse to write our starters. You can begin with these prayers or say your own. You may want to look back at page 8 to see a full description of the A.C.T.S. Prayer Time described in detail.

A (Adoration)
"God, I praise You for inviting me to be Your friend."

C (Confession)
"Jesus, I confess that I do not always follow Your example."

T (Thanksgiving)
"Jesus, thank you for giving me your words in 1 John
so that I can be encouraged today."

S (Supplication)
"Help me to be diligent in my time with You.
Help me to do my Sword Study, tomorrow."

DAY TWO

ON MY KNEES:

Welcome back! Come and join us again. Remember, we always begin by praying.

PRAY

"Jesus, you are my patient teacher. I want to listen to Your words. Help me to learn more about You today."

WRITE

Turn to Psalm 111:10* and carefully read the words. Write verse 10 on the lines below. Did you notice the * next to the verse? The * tells you that there is a Bible Memory Card for this verse in the back of your Sword Study. Use it to memorize the passage! You will find a card in the back of your book.

_____

_____

_____

_____

_____

READ

Are you ready? Today, you do not need to read the whole book of 1 John again. Just read 1 John Chapter 1.

INVESTIGATIVE STUDY
AERIAL VIEW: THE BIG PICTURE

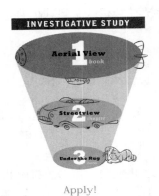

INVESTIGATIVE STUDY

Aerial View book 1

Streetview chapter 2

Under the Rug 3

Apply!

Did you hear John say, "Dear Friends?" Or did he sign his letter, "Love, John?" Nope- John starts right in and never announced himself at the beginning, middle or end!

John wrote 1 John about 60 years after Jesus walked on the earth, around 90 AD. He was older and living in Ephesus when he wrote the letter. Find Ephesus on the map below.

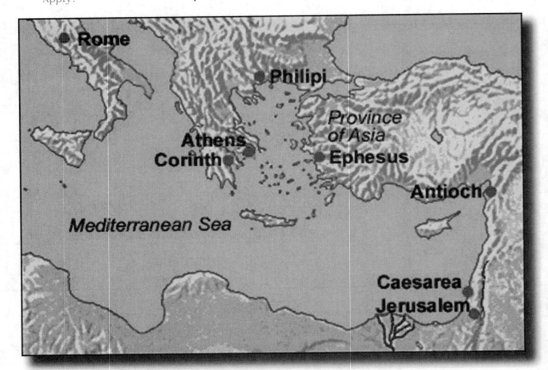

Ephesus was a shipping port near the Mediterranean Sea. It was the capital city of Asia. If you were to look around during his time, you would see forests in the south and orchards to the east. The sea was to the west and fields were in the north. Many of the city people worshipped idols at the huge temple of Artemis/Diana. The temple was known as one of the Seven Wonders of the Ancient World.

Since John gets right to the point in his letter without telling us about himself, we are going to look at other passages to get to know him. Find the verses on the next page and write what you learn about John on the lines.

Matthew 4:21 _____

_____

Matthew 10:1-2 _____

_____

Revelation 1:1, 9-11 _____

_____

Today, we learned that John was a fisherman and one of the first disciples. John became one of Jesus' closest, earthly friends. No wonder Jesus chose John to write a letter about having a true friendship with Jesus, His Father and the family of believers!

A.C.T.S. Prayer Time

Talking to the Lord in prayer is a great part of your friendship with Him. Pray before you close your Sword Study for the day.

A (Adoration)
"Lord, You made the world and everything in it. I praise You for asking me to be Your friend."

C (Confession)
"Lord, I confess that I am not the best friend that I could be. Help me want to spend time listening to You through the Bible."

T (Thanksgiving)
"Thank You, Lord, for being patient with me as I learn about You."

S (Supplication)
"Lord, make the Bible's words important to me. Help me look forward to this time more every day."

DIGGING DEEPER!

Pull out a globe or look at a world map. Ephesus was where Turkey is located today. On the lines below, note the surrounding countries and any current-day details about the region.

_____

_____

_____

_____

D A Y   T H R E E

O N   M Y   K N E E S :

You are doing really well! Each time you return to God's Word, He promises to bless you. Let's begin by praying.

PRAY

"Lord, I know You hear me when I pray. I need to know what is true, so I am studying Your Word. Help me to want to know You more. In Jesus' name, I pray."

WRITE

Turn and read Psalm 119:160. Isn't that a great math problem? All of God's Word equals truth. Write the verse on the lines below.

_____

_____

_____

_____

READ

☺ Do you know what we are going to ask you to do? You are right! Please read 1 John, Chapter 2 now.

INVESTIGATIVE STUDY
AERIAL VIEW: THE BIG PICTURE

INVESTIGATIVE STUDY

Aerial View
book

Streetview
chapter

Under the Rug

Apply!

The World of 1 John

You are flying high above 1 John during this first week of Bible study. We call this the AERIAL VIEW because we are not looking at the details of each verse or chapter. When you are in an airplane, looking down from 20,000 feet, you can only see the big objects on the ground. This is how we are looking at 1 John this week. We have seen the author, where he lived and, now, we will look at the people who were reading his letter.

The Christians of John's day were being confused by false teachers called Gnostics. The teachers were teaching Gnosticism.

Let's start by learning how to say this word! The "G" is silent. So, you say it like this "nos - tick." You have it, "nos - tick." A Gnostic taught false beliefs called Gnosticism.

Next, we can take apart the word. The word Gnostic comes from the word "gnosis," which means "to know." The false teachers said that they had a lot of knowledge and it was special.

We have listed what they were teaching. Under the false, Gnostic sentences, we have given you a verse. Use the line to write out the truth from God's Word.

1. False Teaching: God is only a spirit.

In 1 Timothy 3:16, God's truth says: _____

_____

_____

2.False Teaching: God does not want a friendship with us.

In Exodus 33:11-12, God's truth says: _____

_____

3. False Teaching: Man can save himself.

In Acts 16:30-31, God's truth says: _____

_____

4. False Teaching: Jesus did not die for our sins.

In 1 Corinthians 15:3, God's truth says: _____

_____

The false teachers had John's readers worried and confused. The Christians had not seen Jesus themselves. They trusted Jesus to give them eternal life, but the Gnostic teachers were telling them they weren't saved unless they had more knowledge. They were new and young believers. John wanted his letter to encourage them about their relationship with Jesus.

A.C.T.S. Prayer Time

When you are confused about what is true, you can ask God to help you understand. The verse you wrote today promises that He will answer us when we call to Him. Prayer is calling to God. Let's do that now.

A (Adoration)
"Jesus, thank You for listening to me when I pray."

C (Confession)
"God, I admit I don't trust You enough."

T (Thanksgiving)
"Thank You for showing me the truth in Your Word."

S (Supplication)
"Help me trust in You and Your words."

D A Y   F O U R

ON MY KNEES:

Are you ready to jump right back into your study? First, let's pray!

PRAY

"Lord, You know everything! Help me to learn from Your words. I can't wait to see what You have to teach me today. In Jesus' name, I pray, amen."

WRITE

For every Sword Study we have two Focus Scriptures. The first Focus Scripture passage encourages us to study God's Word, the other is a summary of the book we are studying. Jeremiah 9:23-24* is our first Focus Scripture. Please write Jeremiah 9:23* on the lines below.

_____

_____

_____

_____

_____

READ

1 John Chapters 3 and 4 are your reading assignment for today. Charge!

INVESTIGATIVE STUDY
AERIAL VIEW: THE BIG PICTURE

INVESTIGATIVE STUDY

Aerial View 1 book

Streetview 2

Under the Rug 3

Apply!

John likes to repeat his reasons for writing his letter. He wants to be clear for his readers. He says, "these things I write" 8 times. You are going to go on a hunt to find them. We have listed the verses. We want you to locate them in your Bible and then mark them with a pencil.

1. ☐ Chapter 1, Verse 4   5. ☐ Chapter 2, Verse 14

2. ☐ Chapter 2, Verse 1   6. ☐ Chapter 2, Verse 21

3. ☐ Chapter 2, Verse 12   7. ☐ Chapter 2, Verse 26

4. ☐ Chapter 2, Verse 13   8. ☐ Chapter 5, Verse 13

We see that John is making sure that he is very clear for his readers. He repeats important messages and says why he is writing. He knows that his readers are being confused by false teachers so he shows how he is going to clear things up.

God is so good to us to make sure we understand His love for us. We will learn more as we study 1 John. Then, it will be clearer to us, too!

Reading a verse or two and then using it to pray can be a great way to talk with the Lord. We will give you a verse like the one above each day.

Watch in the A.C.T.S. prayer time how we use it to make our prayer starters. Soon, you will be able to do this on your own.

A.C.T.S. Prayer Time

"The LORD sat as King at the flood; yes, the LORD sits as King forever. The LORD will give strength to His people; The LORD will bless His people with peace."
Psalm 29:10-11 New American Standard Version

A (Adoration)
"God, You are the King of kings. You have ruled over all things forever."

C (Confession)
"Oh, I confess I worry about things in my life. Forgive me for not trusting in Your strength."

T (Thanksgiving)
"Thank You for offering me Your strength and peace."

S (Supplication)
"Dear Jesus, please show me Your strength today. Help me to think about You during the rest of my day."

DAY FIVE

ON MY KNEES:

Wow! Week 1 is coming to an end. Remember, you are growing in God's knowledge every time you pray, write, read and study the Bible. Best of all, you are getting to know God better. Praise Him that He allows you to do this!

PRAY

"Heavenly Father, thank You so much for letting me get to know You. Thank You for the Bible. Please be with me as I study today. In Jesus' name, I pray."

WRITE

Now, you can write the second verse of our first Focus Scripture. Please write Jeremiah 9:24*.

_____

_____

_____

_____

_____

_____

READ

You've made it! WAIT…don't read anything-yet!

INVESTIGATIVE STUDY
AERIAL VIEW: THE BIG PICTURE

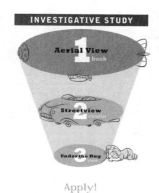

Apply!

We are about to wrap up our investigation from a big-picture view, but before we drop down to a more detailed look at 1 John, let's summarize what you have found so far.

Part of our AERIAL view is to look for a key verse in each chapter. We have listed ours below. We want you to write them on the lines and then make a title (a name for the chapter). This isn't a test! There aren't any perfect titles. We want you to write something that will remind YOU of each chapter.

Start by finding the verse in your Bible and underlining it in your favorite color. Then, write down three or four words from the verse that you think are most important. Finally, name the chapter.

Chapter 1, "_____"

Important words of verse 3:

_____

_____

Chapter 2, "_____"

Important words of verse 13:

_____

_____

Chapter 3, "_____**"**

Important words of verse 1:

_____

_____

Chapter 4, "_____**"**

Important words of verse 10:

_____

_____

Chapter 5, "_____**"**

Important words of verse 13:

_____

_____

A.C.T.S. Prayer Time

"The fear of the LORD is the beginning of wisdom: a good understanding have all they that do his commandments: his praise endureth for ever."

Psalm 111:10 King James Version

A (Adoration)
"Lord, You provide wisdom. You, and You alone, deserve praise forever."

C (Confession)
"Forgive me, Lord, when I don't give You praise. I confess I am not always thankful for what You have given me."

T (Thanksgiving)
"Thank You, Lord, for all the ways You have blessed me."

S (Supplication)
"Give me more of Your understanding and wisdom."

Dwight L. Moody: Light of Chicago

On January 14, 1870, three junior reporters from the River Oaks News Club had the privilege of interviewing Reverend Dwight L. Moody, one of our country's most well-known evangelists. What's an evangelist? Our club wondered that, too, so we sent Alex Thomas (seventeen), Zachary Baker (fourteen) and Hunter Allan (ten) over to Rev. Moody's office in downtown Chicago for some answers. Here's their interview:

Alex: Thanks so much for your time, sir. I know you agreed to meet with us because you like young people. Can you explain?

Moody: For one thing, young man, you should know I was once a young man, too, way back in Northfield, Massachusetts. Hard to believe, isn't it? Did you know I never went past the fifth grade? Stay with your education. It will serve you well.

Zachary: Why did you drop out of school, sir?

Moody: It wasn't a case of dropping out, my friend, but of helping support my family. You see, my father died when I was but four years old. Soon, my mother delivered twins, giving me seven siblings. Once I was strong enough to do a man's work on the farm, Mother urged me to quit school.

Hunter: Reverend Moody, I can't even imagine such hardship. Did you become a farmer?

Moody *(chuckles):* Not for long, son, not for long. You see, I was better at talking to people than to cornstalks. By age seventeen, I said goodbye to the fields and hello to my uncle's shoe business in Boston. Even then, I was in the business of saving soles.

Alex *(laughing):* We heard you had a good sense of humor, sir. Anyway, did you succeed in the shoe business?

Moody: I did well, tolerably well. In fact, I had a goal to become a millionaire. But God did better with me than I did in business.

Zachary: Can you explain, sir?

Moody: That's quite a story, my boy. As one of the requirements for my employment, Uncle Samuel insisted I attend his church. Reluctantly, I went. But before long, my Sunday School teacher, Edward Kimball, visited me in Uncle's shoe shop. He said, "I want to tell you how much Christ loves you." Right then, I knelt to receive Christ's love-gift of salvation and surrendered my soul to Him.

Hunter: Amazing! So is that when you first became a preacher and evangelist?

Moody: No, not quite. At that point, my mind was still more cluttered with dollars than doing God's will. About that time, I made the decision to move to the big city of Chicago. There, I fully intended to make my fortune in the shoe business.

Alex: And did you?

Moody: Praise God, He got hold of me before the money did. I rented a room from a woman I called Mother Phillips. She held me accountable to pray, read my Bible daily and attend church. She also asked me to assist her in city mission work. I began an outreach to the thousands of poor children who roamed Chicago's streets and alleys.

Zach: Is that how you became an evangelist?. We've heard you called "the light of Chicago," but we don't quite understand.

Moody: Well, I bet you're an evangelist, too, my boy—someone who shares the good news of Jesus Christ. That's how I shone my light for the Lord. I started volunteering for the local YMCA (Young Men's Christian Association) while still selling shoes. As my passion for the Lord and His work grew, I held more and more evangelistic meetings, concentrating especially on the youth.

Hunter: Yet people called you "Crazy Moody." Why?

Moody (laughing): I think that came about the time I held a Bible class beside Lake Michigan. The young people sat on driftwood to listen. Some would have called my actions "crazy," I suppose.

Zachary: What other ministries were you involved in, sir?

Moody: One of the first efforts I made became the foundation for the rest.

In 1858, I started a mission Sunday School at North Market Hall in a slum of our fair city.

Hunter: I know what Sunday School is, but what's a "mission" Sunday School? And what's a slum?

Moody: You remind me of myself, young man. So much to learn, and so many questions. No one at the time knew what a mission Sunday School was, either. But some fellow churchgoers promised to allow me to have a Sunday School class if I made my own. So I went out, like the disciples, into the highways and byways—only in my case, it was the alleys and street corners—and brought them in.

Hunter: Brought them in?

Moody: Yes, sir. I brought poor children, all from immigrant families, right into the church and gave them all the Bible teaching I could. And son, you asked about the word "slum." These children lived in places no one should ever have to live. But the first Sunday, eighteen of these children came with me to Sunday School. And we did nothing but grow from there on out.

Alex: Your life was changing fast, wasn't it, sir?

Moody: Yes, indeed. In 1860, I left the business world forever, believing my life should not be spent piling up wealth but helping the less fortunate. Our Sunday School grew to more than 1500 people, and people began urging me to start a church. So on February 28, 1864, the Illinois Street Church opened with me as its pastor.

Even with all their questions, our reporters still haven't finished finding out about Reverend Moody. Stay tuned to next week's Sword Study as they continue their conversation.

DAY ONE

ON MY KNEES:

Be still and know that He is God. Before you rush into your Bible study, slow down and begin with prayer.

PRAY

"God, sometimes I am moving so fast through my day that I don't stop to think about You. Help me to sit here and pay attention to what You are saying in 1 John. I want to be a good student."

WRITE

We have come to a very special point in our writing assignments. Today, you will begin writing your own copy of 1 John. Turn to the "Write!" section in the back of your Sword Study and write 1 John 1:1. Be neat!

READ

Whew! We are now going to drop down to the STREETVIEW, so you only need to read 1 John 1 today.

INVESTIGATIVE STUDY
STREETVIEW: CHAPTER 1

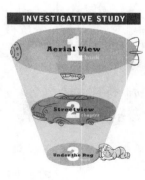

Apply!

At the STREETVIEW, we will look at only one chapter. We will spend the next 10 days digging through the ten verses. We would miss all kinds of great news if we stayed up in the clouds!

Today, we will interview the chapter by quizzing the verses. We will ask "Who, What, Why, When, Where and How" questions for each verse. We will do the first five verses today and the last five tomorrow.

Before we begin though, we need to learn about the "Word of Life." John talks about the Word of Life in Chapter 1 for THREE whole verses!

Turn to John 1:14 in your Bible

What did the Word become, according to John 1:14?_____

What is flesh?_____

Who is the "only begotten of the Father"? _____

      Now that you know, from God's Word, that Jesus is the Word of Life, let's begin our quiz time.

Using 1 John 1:1, circle the items John used to witness the Word of Life:

Ears   **Eyes**   **Hands**   **Feet**

In verse 2, Who was with Jesus in the beginning? _____

In verse 3, Who is the Son of God? _____

In verse 4, What did John want his readers to have? _____

In verse 5, What is God? _____

A.C.T.S. PRAYER TIME

How amazing that God would send His Son, Jesus Christ, for people to hear, see and touch. Close your time with Him in prayer.

A (Adoration)
"God of light, I praise You for sending Your Son to show me Your light."

C (Confession)
"Father, I admit that I don't walk in the ways You want me to live."

T (Thanksgiving)
"Thank You for giving me Your power to walk in the light."

S (Supplication)
"God, help me to be quick to confess my sins to You."

DIGGING DEEPER!

We are going to bring you on a treasure hunt to find out more about Jesus.

The story of the Word becoming flesh is told in Luke 2. Read the whole chapter, then go back and read the gospel of John, Chapter 1. After you have read these two chapters, read 1 John 1:1-3. Finally, read Genesis 1:1. Isn't that a great mini-treasure hunt? Write a short summary of what you learned from your hunt on the lines below.

_____

_____

_____

_____

_____

D A Y   T W O

O N   M Y   K N E E S :

Come, faithful friend of the Word. Are you settled in and ready to be encouraged by God's words? Begin by going to your Heavenly Father in prayer.

PRAY

"Father, it is so good to know You hear me when I pray. I want to be refreshed in Your Word today. Teach me new understanding and give me strength, to live out what I learn. In Jesus' name, I pray, amen."

WRITE

Turn to the "My Copy of 1 John" section and copy 1 John 1:2.

READ

Once again, read 1 John 1 before moving to the INVESTIGATIVE STUDY section.

I N V E S T I G A T I V E   S T U D Y
S T R E E T   V I E W : C H A P T E R 1

Apply!

Okay, let's finish interviewing the 1 John, Chapter 1 verses. Remember to use the words from your Bible in your answers.

In verse 6, what are we doing if we say we have fellowship with God, but walk in the darkness?

_____

In verse 7, what does Jesus' blood do for us?

_____

In verse 8, what is not in us if we say we have no sin?

_____

In verse 9, what does God do if we confess our sins?

_____

In verse 9, what two things do we find out about God?

He is _____ and _____.

In verse 10, what is not in us if we say that we have not sinned?

_____

Before we wrap up our INVESTIGATIVE STUDY section today, we want to show you one more way to dig deeper for more understanding in a Bible chapter. You can look for comparisons, or look for two things that are opposite. John uses two comparisons in 1 John 1. Fill in the blanks below.

Comparisons of 1 John 1

In verse 5, "light" is compared to: _____

In verse 6, "lie" is compared to: _____

John has used these two comparisons to show us how different people live their lives. God wants His children to live in His ways, which are compared to walking in the light. We will learn more about this as we study 1 John. Maybe you will play some light and dark games during your family's Bonfire time!

APPLY!

When others look at how you chose to act, do they see an example of what Jesus would do? Match the Christ-like behavior to the opposite behavior. Next, circle with a red colored pencil the ones that are examples of how Jesus would want you to live.

Unkind	Encouraging
Complaining	Kind
Discouraging	Content
Harsh	Agreeable
Arguementative	Gentle

A.C.T.S. Prayer Time

"The steadfast love of the Lord never ceases; his mercies never come to an end; they are new every morning; great is your faithfulness."
Lamentations 3:22-23 English Standard Version

Praise the Lord that He is willing to forgive us when we don't live the way we should! How great it is to realize that we can start every day with new mercy!

A (Adoration)
"God of the past, present and future, You are awesome and great."

C (Confession)
"I confess there are days that I don't think about You first."

T (Thanksgiving)
"Thank you, Jesus, for loving me before I loved You."

S (Supplication)
"Help me to think about how I act today. I want to live the way You want me to live."

DAY THREE

ON MY KNEES:

Did you see the sun rise this morning? You don't have to get up that early, but starting your day with Jesus is the best way to begin a day. Let's pray.

PRAY

"Heavenly Father, I come to You because I know Your Son, Jesus. I want our time together to be the most important event of my day. Show me how I can be a better child of Yours."

WRITE

Carefully write 1 John 1:3 in the "Write!" section of your study.

READ

Keep your Bible open to 1 John, stand up and boldly read Chapter 1 out loud.

INVESTIGATIVE STUDY
STREET VIEW: CHAPTER 1

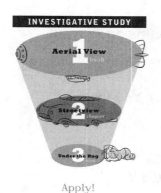

Apply!

Do you have a nickname? Does someone you know have a nickname? Maybe your name is Abigail, but people call you Abby. Or, maybe your name is Alexander, but people call you Alex.

John wrote the gospel book of John. It is a much longer book than his letter of 1 John. Sometimes he uses phrases from his book of John or other writings of the New Testament. He expected his readers to know what he was talking about so he shortened some of his phrases, similar to how we use nicknames.

Today, we are going to read a phrase in 1 John and then look at other verses to help us understand John's letter. Look up the verse under the phrase and then write a note to yourself about what you learn.

"From the beginning…" in Verse 1

John 1:1 _____

John 17:5 _____

"What we heard, saw and touched/handled…" in Verse 1

John 1:14 _____

Luke 24:39 _____

_____

"Eternal life…" in Verse 2

John 17:3* _____

1 John 5:13* _____

"Darkness…" in Verse 5

John 1:1-5 _____

_____

John 3:19-21 _____

Ephesians 5:8 _____

A.C.T.S. Prayer Time

"The Lord opens the eyes of the blind; The Lord raises up those who are bowed down; The Lord loves the righteous; The Lord protects the strangers; He supports the fatherless and the widow, But He thwarts the way of the wicked."
Psalm 146:8-9 New American Standard Version

A (Adoration)
"Father, I praise You for being my perfect Father. You always give me what is good."

C (Confession)

"Lord, I confess that as I think through my day yesterday, I need to repent of my sin of _____."

T (Thanksgiving)

"Thank you for forgiving me all of my sins and then giving me eternal life in Your Son and making me Your child."

S (Supplication)

"Lord, help me understand 1 John. Help its truths change me from the inside out so I will live like You want me to live."

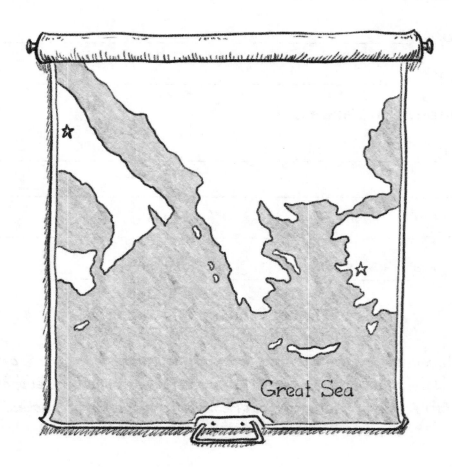

Great Sea

D A Y   F O U R

ON MY KNEES:

Be of good cheer! God is waiting for you. Isn't it amazing that the God who made the whole universe loves you and wants to meet with YOU! He does not force us to come. He does not demand us to sit. He patiently waits on His children to come. How incredible! Begin in prayer before studying His Word.

PRAY

"Lord, You are amazing! Share more of what You are like with me. Help me to stay focused during our time together."

WRITE

Open your Scriptures to 1 John 1:4 and think about the words as you write them out in your Sword Study pages.

READ

Before we begin a new level of study, read through the first chapter of 1 John.

INVESTIGATIVE STUDY
STREET VIEW: CHAPTER 1

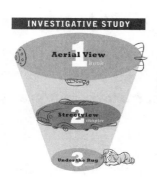

Apply!

Are you ready for a few more verses that explain John's phrases in 1 John?

If God had wanted, He could have given us a library of books about Himself that would have overflowed the earth (John 21:25).

Instead, He gave us just 66 mini-books in one Bible. Each of these verses will give you additional information. Be sure to gather as much as possible from each one and write down what you find.

"God is light..." in Verse 5

John 8:12*_____

_____

Psalm 27:1_____

"He is in the light..." in Verse 7

Matthew 5:14-16_____

_____

"We make Him a liar..." in Verse 10

Numbers 23:19_____

Titus 1:1-3_____

A.C.T.S. Prayer Time

"Sing aloud unto God our strength: make a joyful noise unto the God of Jacob."
Psalm 81:1 King James Version

Joy! John wanted his letter to bring us joy. Being able to fellowship with the God of Creation and His Son forever should bring us LOTS of joy! Let's praise Him in prayer as we finish.

A (Adoration)
"Hallelujah! God of wonder, what a joy that I am able to come into Your presence, and have a friendship with You."

C (Confession)
"Forgive me, Father, for times I make You wait and don't make our time the most important part of my day."

T (Thanksgiving)
"Thank you, Lord, for allowing me in Your holy presence. Thank You for wanting a close friendship with me."

S (Supplication)
"Give me a craving to fellowship with You through the Bible every day."

DAY FIVE

ON MY KNEES:

We have finished Week 2. Are you getting used to coming here every day? Let's pray.

PRAY

"Holy, Holy, Holy is Your Name! Jesus, thank You for inviting me to study Your words. Help me to sit quietly and learn wisdom from Your Word. In Your holy name, I pray."

WRITE

John 1:5-6 talk about the differences between the light and dark. Write the verses in your "Write" pages.

READ

Slowly read 1 John 1. Don't speed through the chapter just because you have read the words before.

INVESTIGATIVE STUDY
UNDER THE RUG: WORD STUDIES

Apply!

We are going down another level today! We have soared in the clouds, lowered to the ground and now we will go UNDER THE RUG. This section of the INVESTIGATIVE STUDY is one of the most exciting parts of your Sword Study!

UNDER THE RUG has two parts: Word Studies and Cross-references.

Today, we will give you a summary of the Word Study process. The Bible was not written in English. This is why we do Word Studies. As we study words in the original languages of the Bible, we can understand better what God meant by them. Here is how we will do word studies:

Word Study:

In **PART A:** We will choose one or two key words from the chapter of 1 John. Then, in the Strong's Concordance we will discover its Strong's number. This will lead us to the Greek word for our English Key Word.

In **PART B:** We will look up the Strong's number in a Greek dictionary to find out more details of the word's meaning in Greek.

In **PART C:** We will choose the correct meaning for the use of the word in 1 John.

Don't worry, we will walk you step-by-step through this process. First, we are going to look at 1 John, Chapter 1 and highlight some key words. Key Words are words that are repeated or a main word that the author is focusing on in the chapter.

We always consider references to God, Jesus and the Holy Spirit as Key Words. Using your Bible, look back over 1 John, Chapter 1 and mark the words below. Sometimes, it is easier to put the symbols around the word or in the margin of your Bible. On your hand-written copy, you may have space to put the symbols above the word.

△ - God, the Father   △ - God, the Son   △ - God, the Spirit
☺ - Fellowship   ☀ - Light   □ - Sin

Now, turn to your handwritten copy of 1 John. Mark the same words for just the first six verses you have copied in your "Write" pages. From now on, when you write in your copy of 1 John, be sure to mark all references to God with the symbols above.

God gave us the Bible so you can know how to have a relationship with Him. After that, it is all about your friendship (fellowshipping) with Him through His Word. He has filled the Scriptures with evidences of what He is like so you can get to know Him.

A.C.T.S. Prayer Time

"For it is you who light my lamp; the Lord my God lightens my darkness....This God— his way is perfect; the word of the Lord proves true; he is a shield for all those who take refuge in him." Psalm 18:28 & 30 English Standard Version

A (Adoration)
"You are my light and Your ways are perfect. Thank You for showing me how to avoid darkness."

C (Confession)
"Forgive me for going not to you for refuge."

T (Thanksgiving)
"Thank You for providing protection for me."

S (Supplication)
"Teach me to run to you in prayer when I am unsure of what to do."

Dwight L. Moody: Light to Chicago (continued)

(We now present the conclusion of a January 14, 1870, interview with the Reverend Dwight L. Moody with three junior reporters from the River Oaks News Club. Let's see if Alex Thomas, Zachary Baker and Hunter Allan can learn more about the Christian life as they explore more about the Reverend D.L. Moody.)

Alex: You began your ministry with a mission Sunday School, and then it grew to become a church. Is that correct, Rev. Moody?

Moody: It is. But the story doesn't end there. The War Between the States lay ahead. And when the Union Army set up Camp Douglas outside Chicago, I realized that God had soldiers, too.

Zachary: What did you do?

Moody: We set up groups to minister to the fighting men. I traveled throughout the state and then the country to reach them for Christ.

Hunter: What do you mean by "reach"?

Moody: Another great question, my young friend. I showed the men how their sin—the wrongs they had done—separated them from God. Then I showed them how to repent and surrender to a full faith in Christ, who died on the cross to cleanse them from sin. I prayed with men from both sides, teaching and allowing the Holy Spirit to lead them to a knowledge of Him.

Alex: Now I understand! You used the war as an opportunity for evangelism.

Moody: Yes, indeed. God can use even sad times to draw people to Himself. The same thing happened with the fire.

Zachary: Oh! I know what you're talking about! The Great Chicago Fire, right?

Moody *(with sadness)*: Yes. When the Fire came, our family lost almost everything—but, praise God, not what was most precious. My wife and three children were fine. But the loss of our church buildings made me realize I had made plans and then asked God to help me with them. From that point on, I surrendered to His desires. I would preach His Word to the world.

Hunter: Missions! That means you did missions, right?

Moody: Yes, my boy. My musician friend Ira Sankey and I, along with our wives, traveled to the United Kingdom, where we held many evangelistic crusades. God used us to help bring about revival in that part of the world. Thousands upon thousands came to each crusade, from England to Ireland to Scotland and back again. We were honored to serve as His messengers.

Alex: I have a quote from you during that time (reading): "I know perfectly well that, wherever I go and preach, there are many better preachers . . . than I am; all that I can say about it is that the Lord uses me."

Moody: Yes, that sounds like something I would have said, son. I can take no credit for the Lord's work.

Zach: And when you returned to the United States, you continued your crusades, right?

Moody: That's correct. We toured the East coast to share the gospel of Christ and also held a crusade in our beloved Chicago. It lasted for sixteen weeks, and as many as 10,000 people came to know the Lord.

Hunter: So people came to know Christ back in the United States, too?

Moody (chuckles): Indeed they did, my boy. Indeed they did.

Alex: And there's more. Before long, you began a new ministry through Bible education, Reverend Moody. You opened the Northfield Seminary for Young Women and the Mount Hermon School for Boys in your home state of Massachusetts. Is that correct, sir?

Moody: It is. I consider these some of my most important avenues of kingdom work.

Zachary: But why schools, Rev. Moody?

Moody: I wanted to train young people to continue the work of reaching the inner city for Christ. Here, they could experience true fellowship as they prepared for Him to use them in great ways. We also began a summer conference ministry, for which we brought in some wonderful Bible teachers and preachers.

Hunter: So you were training average people to do great things?

Moody: Yes, indeed. As I said at the time, "If this world is going to be reached, I am convinced that it must be done by men and women of average talent. After all, there are comparatively few people who have great talents." God can do wonderful work through hearts surrendered and trained to share His good news.

Alex: And that's just what you saw happen.

Moody: That's right. The gospel was shared at home and abroad. Our school at Mount Hermon, for example, helped birth what became known as the Student Volunteer Movement for Foreign Missions.

Zachary: I read about that! As the result of this movement, thousands of young people have begun volunteering to serve Christ overseas.

Moody: Yes. But I am growing old, and the work remains unfinished. I find myself asking the Father what else I can do, what further legacy I can leave. Not long ago, the Lord led me to open the Chicago Bible Institute, an even more extensive ministry training school than the two in Massachusetts.

Hunter: I know the Lord will guide you in His way.

Moody: To be sure, young man, to be sure.

Alex: Thank you for speaking with us today, Reverend Moody. We will pray with you about the future needs in Chicago and throughout the world. Thank you for all you've shared with us and with the many who have come to know Christ because of your faithfulness.

Moody: Long ago, I heard the British evangelist Henry Varley say, "It remains to be seen what the Lord can do with a man wholly consecrated to Christ." From then on, I determined to be such a man. And that is my prayer for you three as well.

Alex, Zachary and Hunter: Thank you, sir! God be with you, sir.

DAY ONE

ON MY KNEES:

Welcome to a brand new week! Before we dig in to our word study, let's go to the Lord in prayer.

PRAY

"Heavenly Father, help me to understand that You are a holy God, righteous in all ways. In Jesus' name, amen."

WRITE

Begin this week's writing by copying 1 John 1:7 in your "Write!" section.

READ

Start your week by re-reading 1 John 1.

INVESTIGATIVE STUDY
UNDER THE RUG: WORD STUDY - "FELLOWSHIP"

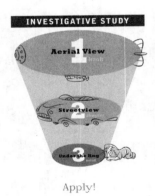

Apply!

In the first chapter of 1 John, we choose **fellowship** and **sin** as the Key Words. We will start with **fellowship**. We are going to do the three word study steps with you.

What do you think of when someone says **fellowship**? Do you think of food and friends? We are going to learn what the Bible means when it says we have **fellowship** with God and His people.

PART A: We looked up the word **fellowship** in Strong's Concordance. The Strong's number assigned to it is 2842. Below is the way the word is written in English, the pronunciation, and the basic definition from the Strong's dictionary:

2842. Fellowship, <u>koinonia</u>. koy-nohn-ee'-ah, noun; from 2844, partnership, i.e. participation, communion.

PART B: Next, we looked up the number in another Greek dictionary:

Fellowship
      1) Communion, sharing in common
      2) An associate, partaker, synonym of fellow traveler

PART C: Now, we will take a second look at how *fellowship* is used in 1 John. This word is only used twelve times in the Bible. It appears four times in 1 John. Let's look at where he used this word and answer a few questions.

Fellowship is in 1 John 1:3 twice; who is *fellowshipping* the first time?

_____

Who are the three people *fellowshipping* the second time the word *fellowship* is mentioned? _____

In 1 John 1:6, when does *fellowship* with God stop? _____

According to 1 John 1:7, who is *fellowshipping* together? _____

     True *fellowship* is so energizing! When we visit with friends that believe in Jesus as their Savior we have a different friendship than with the friends we have that don't trust in Jesus. We can also help one another walk in the right way, in the light!

A.C.T.S. Prayer Time

Open your Bible and turn to John 8:12*. What Jesus says about Himself is a perfect summary of 1 John 1:7, isn't it?

A (Adoration)
"You are the Light of the world, and in You there is no darkness."

C (Confession)
"Lord, forgive me for making the wrong choices and walking in the dark."

T (Thanksgiving)
"Thank You, Lord, for showing me how to walk in Your light."

S (Supplication)
"Lord, help me to walk in Your light and tell others about You."

D A Y   T W O

On My Knees:

Keep up the great dedication!

PRAY

"Jesus, You see everything and care for me. Help me hear Your words and not my thoughts. Amen."

WRITE

Copy 1 John 1:8 onto the next lines of your "My Copy of 1 John" pages.

READ

Please read 1 John 1 without hurrying.

INVESTIGATIVE STUDY
UNDER THE RUG: Cross References - "Fellowship"

Apply!

Let's look at **fellowship** around the Bible and see what there is to learn about our **fellowship** with Christ and others.

Read Acts 2:42, then answer the questions below:

Who was **fellowshipping** in this passage? _____

What did they do together? _____

_____

Read 2 Corinthians 13:11-14, then answer the questions on the next page:

What does Paul tell the believers to do? (list all) _____

_____

What *fellowship* does John 1:14 proclaim? _____

A.C.T.S. Prayer Time

"For I know that in me (that is, in my flesh,) dwelleth no good thing: for to will is present with me; but how to perform that which is good I find not."
Romans 7:18 King James Version

A (Adoration)
"Lord, You are the Way, the Truth and the Life. You are my power to fight sin."

C (Confession)
"Lord, I am sorry that I make the wrong choices and don't follow Your ways."

T (Thanksgiving)
"Thank You for Your Word that teaches me."

S (Supplication)
"Lord, when I do sin, help me to be quick to confess and return to You."

Digging Deeper!

Did you notice the additional symbols in the left margin of your "Write!" page? The symbols for God, the Father, Son and Holy Spirit have been placed on each page. They are there for you to write a three or four-word note about what you learn about God. Go ahead and do this for your first eight verses.

NOTE! Do not interrupt your copying time to note what you learn about God in the margin- do that after you have finished copying the verses you have been assigned.

DAY THREE

ON MY KNEES:

Welcome back! Sometimes we look at our Bible study like schoolwork. Please don't do that! Our time with Jesus should not be like a school assignment. Our time with Jesus is like meeting with a good friend for a visit. Let's talk with Him, now.

PRAY

"Heavenly Father, my time with You is special. Help me to learn how to depend on You. Amen."

WRITE

1 John 1:9 is a powerful verse. Copy it on your pages in a unique way, perhaps in cursive or a different color.

READ

Stand up. Walk to a place outdoors, if possible. Read 1 John 1 standing up, like you are reading a letter to a group of people.

INVESTIGATIVE STUDY
UNDER THE RUG: WORD STUDY - "SIN"

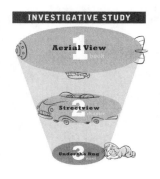

S-I-N. We don't hear this word often.

Do you remember when John compared light and dark? Darkness is when **sin** is around. The light doesn't have **sin**. We are to walk in the light. **Sin** breaks our fellowship with God. **Sin** does not break our **relationship** with God. We are still His children if we **sin**.

We must have a relationship with God BEFORE we can fellowship. Our trust in Jesus as our Savior gives us our relationship with God, and then we can fellowship with Him. **Sin** is why we need a Savior. Everyone needs Jesus as their Savior or they cannot be friends with God.

Over the next few days, we will see what God's Word says about **sin**. First, let's see what the definition of **sin** is in Greek through our word studies.

PART A: We looked up word **sin** in Strong's Concordance and found out Strong's numbers are 264 and 266. Below are the English words, how to pronounce the words, and the simple definitions from the Strong's dictionary:

> **264. Sin.** <u>hamartano</u> Ham-ar-tan'-o, verb; to miss the mark, to err, offend, trespass.
> **266. Sin.** <u>hamartia</u>, ham-ar-tee'-ah, noun; from 264: offense, sin(-ful).

PART B: Next, we looked up the numbers 264 and 266 in another Greek dictionary. We discovered more details and ways the word **sin** is used in the Bible.

264. Sin, verb; To do wrong.
    1) Sinning against God
        A) The act of sinning, 1 John 1:10, 2:1
        B) Practicing sin, 1 John 3:6 (twice), 1 John 3:8, 9.
        C) Present tense indicates the condition resulting from an act, such as "unto death," 1 John 5:16

266. Sin, noun; A wrong-doing to God that makes us guilty.
    1) Wandering from the truth
    2) Wandering from the law or rules

PART C: Now, go back to 1 John 1 in your Bible and put a ☹ above (or in your Bible's margin) the words **sin** or **sinned**.

A.C.T.S. Prayer Time

"Create in me a clean heart, O God; and renew a right spirit within me."
Psalm 51:10 English Standard Version

A (Adoration)
"God, only You can clear my sin. You are holy and cannot look upon sin."

C (Confession)
"Jesus, forgive me for the ways that I have chosen to sin today."

T (Thanksgiving)
"Thank You, Jesus, for cleaning my heart of sin and making it as white as snow."

S (Supplication)
"Please help me to walk through today in a right way."

D A Y   F O U R

ON MY KNEES:

Coming to Jesus each day gives us wisdom. Did you know that wisdom means knowledge or understanding? The only perfect wisdom comes from God's Word. Start today asking for His wisdom.

PRAY

"Lord, I am getting used to meeting with You each day. I am seeing more and more how to walk in Your light. Give me more of Your wisdom today. In Jesus' name, I pray. Amen."

WRITE

Hooray! One more verse and you have written the first chapter of 1 John! Copy verse 10 on your "Write!" page.

READ

Now, read your own handwritten copy of 1 John 1 before beginning the INVESTIGATIVE STUDY section.

INVESTIGATIVE STUDY
UNDER THE RUG: CROSS REFERENCES - "SIN"

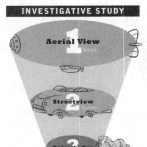

Understanding the definitions of **sin** is VERY important.

God is light and He does not fellowship in the darkness.

God sees either Jesus and there is fellowship, or He sees **sin** and there is no fellowship. If we have believed in Jesus as our payment, then we have been saved from the penalty of **sin**, which is death.

Before we do cross references of the word **sin**, let's make certain that we have a **relationship** with God.

According to Romans 3:23, who has **sinned?** _____

According to Romans 6:23, what is the penalty of **sin?** _____

According to 1 Peter 2:21-25, who died for our **sins?** _____

According to Romans 10:9-10, what must we do to be saved? _____

_____

_____

According to Hebrews 10:26-27, what happens to the person who keeps **sinning** after hearing the truth of God's salvation?

_____

      Have you begun your **relationship** with God through Jesus? If your answer is yes, then when we walk in the light, we enjoy fellowship with the Lord and His people. We experience joy like John was excitedly sharing in 1 John.

APPLY!

Are you wondering if you have a personal relationship with God? Talk with a parent about your questions. Ask him or her to share with you the story of the day he or she began a relationship with God.

A.C.T.S. Prayer Time

"My little children, I am writing these things to you so that you may not sin. And if anyone sins, we have an Advocate with the Father, Jesus Christ the righteous;"

1 John 2:1 New American Standard Version

A (Adoration)

"Jesus, I praise Your Holy name. You had power over sin and paid my penalty!"

C (Confession)

"Lord, I struggle with wanting to do the wrong things."

T (Thanksgiving)

"Thank You for Your love that made a way for me to be with You forever."

S (Supplication)

"Lord, give me Your power and strength to choose not to sin."

DAY FIVE

ON MY KNEES:

Today brings us to a very special activity in our Sword Study. We have been waiting for you to arrive here! Begin in prayer first.

PRAY.

"Lord, You are my God. I want to learn more about what You want by studying Your Word. I want to be a close friend of Yours. Please help me gladly spend time with You."

WRITE.

Look back over your copy of 1 John. Mark any references to God with the symbols we have given you.

READ.

Take a little break from reading 1 John today!

INVESTIGATIVE STUDY
1-2-3 SUMMARIZE: CHAPTER 1

Congratulations! You have finished the INVESTIGATIVE STUDY of the first chapter of 1 John. We have a neat way for you to wrap up all that you have been learning over the last two weeks.

At the end of this day, you will see a "Day 10 Diagram." Around the edges of the picture, there are blanks for you to fill out. In the center, the Day 10 Diagram will have a picture that summarizes the chapter. If you have any problems figuring out how to fill in your Day 10 Diagram, talk to a parent; the Parent Guidebook includes the answer key to this diagram.

☐ To begin, look at the top of the Day 10 Diagram. Fill in the chapter number. Look at Week 1, Day 5 for the original title you created for 1 John 1. Review what you wrote and refine your title with the new insights that you have learned over the last 10 days.

☐ Next, which verse from the chapter do you think was the "key verse?"

☐ On the right of the page, transfer your key Greek words from this chapter. Write the English words on the top line after the words "Greek Words." Transfer the Greek spellings and write a short definition of their meanings.

☐ On the bottom of the Diagram page, transfer the most important things that you learned about God through marking the references about Him on your "Write!" pages.

You've observed how strongly John emphasizes the difference between light and darkness, so you won't be surprised to see two contrasting areas in this summary drawing of 1 John 1. As you study the diagram, look for the beloved disciple John standing near a map of Asia. On the blank above John's head, write the name of the city from which he wrote the letter of 1 John. Then, on the lines to the right of John, note four things that you learned about him through your studies these past two weeks.

Thunder clouds of false teaching were looming over the people of Asia in John's day. On the line in the stormy sky, write the name of the untrue belief system from which John wished to protect the believers. Though the dark clouds seem huge and threatening, God has provided a path into His light by way of the cross of Christ. What did we learn was nailed to the cross so that we could live forever with God? Fill in the note on the cross and thank God once again for his amazing gift of grace! Write the Greek words for sin on each side of the middle beam of the cross.

Now, on the open Bible at the top of the cross, write the name that John called Jesus in verse 1:1. Our fellow believers in the diagram have crossed from the darkness into the light of eternal life with Christ through the cross. Write the Greek word for "fellow travelers" above the heads of Sword Study travelers. Mark the lighthouse on the mountainside with one characteristic that John says in Chapter 1 that God is, and two characteristics that God is not.

Remember that John also said that he was proclaiming a joyful message about the new fellowship that is possible for those who have put their faith in Christ? Just like the recipients of John's letter, our belief in Christ's finished work of the cross makes it possible for us to enjoy an ongoing love relationship with others. Under the lighthouse, write the word, "Fellowship," and then list those with whom John says we can now have fellowship. You can enjoy that fellowship this week as you meet with the Lord each day, and as you gather with your family and friends who also know Jesus.

Now that you have completed your Diagram, take a few moments to consider the full picture. Be sure to share your thoughts with your family during the Family Bonfire time this week.

A.C.T.S. Prayer Time

"The LORD is good unto them that wait for him, to the soul that seeketh him."
Lamentations 3:25 King James Version

A (Adoration)
"Lord, thank You for being so good to me all the time."

C (Confession)
"Lord, I am sorry that I complain about what You allow to come into my life."

T (Thanksgiving)
"Thank You, Lord, for being patient with me as I learn."

S (Supplication)
"Lord, I want to seek You, but sometimes I am lazy. Help me to come to study no matter how I feel."

Title: _____
Key Verse: _____

Chapter: _____ : _____

Greek Words: _____

Asia

Samuel Morris: Light out of the Jungle
(Speech given at Taylor University Convocation, September 9, 1892)

As I look out upon you today, I see before me my fellow students as well as professors, staff and benefactors of Taylor University. But today, I call you my friends. And since you are my friends, I will share something most dear and precious: the story of the Lord God Almighty's great working in my life.

Like most of you, I did not begin my life in a university setting. But unlike most of you, I did not start out in this beautiful country, or even one you would consider civilized. My life began far from our fair city of Fort Wayne, Indiana.

Instead, it began in the heart of the jungle on the dark continent of Africa. I was born Prince Kaboo, son of a chieftain in the country you know as Liberia. There, I lived a simple life, a good life of family, hunting and tribal celebrations. A good life, that is, until war overtook our land and our people.

The debts of war mounted. One day, an enemy chief came to my father and demanded payback. "If you want peace, you must pay," he thundered.

"We will pay. We will pay!" my father pleaded.

"Yes, you will. You will pay with your son." Our opponent's words split the air—and my heart. Rough arms grabbed me from behind. Suddenly, I was a hostage, bound to the enemy until our tribe could pay its debts.

My father delivered gift after gift to the enemy chief. None brought satisfaction. "No," the wicked leader roared. "It will take more than that to pay what you owe."

Every day, he whipped me with a thorny, poisonous vine. Its venom soon infected the welts on my back, and I grew weak and sick. What would become of me?

I overheard my captors: "We're tired of waiting. His father had better bring enough goods this time, or we'll bury him alive." I could no longer stand, so they tied me to a wooden cross and prepared to beat me one last time.

I couldn't respond. I didn't care. All I wanted was relief from this unbearable pain—even if it meant death. As I hung over the grave they had prepared for me, I could feel my life slipping away.

Suddenly, a bright light shone all around me. The knots untwisted. The ropes fell off my hands and feet. Then I heard it: "Kaboo!" Weak as I was, the voice pierced my heart. "RUN!" The weakness dropped away as fast as the ropes had. Strength filled my body. I could stand. I could run! I bounded into the jungle as fast as I could, hiding in a hollow tree until darkness fell.

As I waited in the tree, I pondered the day's events. Who had spoken to me? What was the light? And what was happening to me now? I had no answers, but I knew the voice spoke truth. I must leave, and quickly. If I returned home to my tribe, the enemy would kill not just me, but all my people.

Once darkness blanketed the jungle, I climbed out of the tree and again stood amazed. The bright light that led me to the tree shone once more. It lit the path before me, guiding me through the night and toward safety.

After many days of walking, I reached a coffee plantation. "Welcome," said a worker, offering to take me to his boss. They needed more laborers. Before I knew it, I had a job and brand-new clothes.

Soon, I noticed something different about the young man who had found me. I often found him kneeling on the floor. "What are you doing?" I asked.

"Praying to God, my Father in heaven," he answered. "Would you like to come with me to church? There, you can learn more about Him."

As I attended the church, I recognized God's presence. A missionary and graduate of Fort Wayne University (now Taylor) spoke on the conversion of the Apostle Paul. In his story, I recognized my own.

Everything began to fit together in my head and heart. God was the bright light. God had brought me out of captivity, out of the jungle and into my new home. And now, God would be my Master, the ruler and guide of my life.

That day, I repented of my sin and received Christ as my Savior and Lord.

In obedience to the Bible, God's holy Book, I was baptized. An American missionary gave me the name of his sponsor, Samuel Morris. I was no longer Kaboo. The old things had passed away. Everything had become new.

But somehow, I couldn't help but wonder: Where would God take me next?

Read the conclusion of Samuel Morris' exciting speech next week!

DAY ONE

ON MY KNEES:

Perfect goodness and justice are found in the Lord. We are a blessed people who know this truth. We can walk in the light as He shows us. Come let us rejoice in His name and exalt in His righteousness. These are words like those you hear in Psalm 89:14-16. Go to Jesus in prayer before you begin studying His words.

PRAY

"Lord, fill my heart with Your joy. Help me to understand all that I study today so that I can rejoice in Your name all day long. Remind me of Your words today so that I will walk in righteousness."

WRITE

Please write 1 John 2:1-3. Say the words as you write them.

READ

Begin this week by reading Chapters 1 & 2 of 1 John.

INVESTIGATIVE STUDY
STREETVIEW: CHAPTER 2

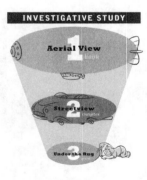

In the first chapter of 1 John, John explained the importance of knowing Jesus and that Jesus came to give us fellowship with God, the Father and Himself and other Christians.

Now, we will focus on the second chapter of 1 John. Over and over, John tells us why he is writing. Be sure to watch for the "why's" as you read each day.

We are going to dig into 1 John, Chapter 2 by reading a verse and then picking five or six words that we think are the most important. The words don't have to be all in a row. We could do all 29 verses, but that might take a really long time, so we will let you choose any eight verses today and then another ten tomorrow. If you want to do all 29, count it as a DIGGING DEEPER activity!

Follow our lead; we have done the first two verses. This may be harder than it looks. It might be fun to do it with a brother, sister or parent!

Verse 1: <u>Jesus is your Advocate if you sin.</u>

Verse 2: <u>Jesus is the world's payment for sins.</u>

Verse __: _____

Verse __: _____

Verse __: _____

Verse __: _____

Verse __: _____

Verse __: _____

Verse __: _____

Verse __: _____

Way to go! You are doing a great job of investigating 1 John, Chapter 2 by reading and writing the most important words. When we go over and over God's Word, He faithfully teaches us. Let's close in prayer to the greatest teacher of all!

A.C.T.S. Prayer Time

*"Now unto the King eternal, immortal, invisible, the only wise God,
be honor and glory forever and ever. Amen."* 1 Timothy 1:17 King James Version

A (Adoration)
"Dear Lord, You are the King of kings."

C (Confession)
"I am sorry for..."

T (Thanksgiving)
"Thank You for..."

S (Supplication)
"Please help me to remember to give you honor and thanks throughout today."

D A Y   T w o

On My Knees:

Where are you today? Are you at your own house or away in a different location? Go before the Lord in prayer, asking for a time of fellowship with Him without any interruptions.

PRAY

"God, I know that You are able to protect, guide and love me perfectly. I want to learn more about You so that I love You more than I do now. Please help me pay attention no matter what is going on around me. Amen."

WRITE

As you write 1 John 2:4-6, remember to mark any mention of God that you find with the symbols you learned earlier.

READ

Diligently read 1 John, Chapter 2.

INVESTIGATIVE STUDY
StreetView: CHAPTER 2

INVESTIGATIVE STUDY

1 Aerial View
book

3 Streetview
Chapter

3 Under the Rug

Apply!

Welcome back! We are going to finish writing important words for the last half of your Chapter 2 verses. Charge!

Verse __: _____

_____

Verse __: _____

_____

Verse __: _____

_____

Verse __: _____

Verse __: _____

Verse __: _____

Verse __: _____

Verse __: _____

Verse __: _____

Verse __: _____

Great job! We know that sometimes these assignments can seem hard, but just like it takes practice to be really good at a sport or a musical instrument, it takes effort to learn about the Lord. And, knowing Him is the most important thing in life. Press on!

A.C.T.S. Prayer Time

"Remember the former things of old: for I am God, and there is none else; I am God, and there is none like me, declaring the end from the beginning, and from ancient times the things that are not yet done, saying, My counsel shall stand, and I will do all my pleasure:" Isaiah 46:9-10 King James Version

Going forward, we would like you to fill in your own "mini" prayer journal in the A.C.T.S. letters below. We will give you a passage to help begin your prayer time. Try to include what God has spoken to you during your study.

A (Adoration)

"Dear Lord, You are..._____"

C (Confession)

"I am sorry for..._____"

T (Thanksgiving)

"Thank You for..._____"

S (Supplication)

"Please help me..._____"

DIGGING DEEPER!

Here are the blank verse lines if you would like to come up with five or six words for the rest of the 1 John, Chapter 2 verses.

Verse ___: _____

Verse ___: _____

Verse ___: _____

Verse ___: _____

Verse ___: _____

Verse ___: _____

Verse ___: _____

Verse ___: _____

Verse ___: _____

DAY THREE

ON MY KNEES:

Being able to pray to the Creator of the universe is no small thing. God could have placed us on earth and then not cared when we were sad, happy, mad or glad. Let us go to Him in prayer before digging in His Word.

PRAY

"Lord, calm my thoughts as I start my study today. I want to stay focused on You, so please help my thoughts from wandering."

WRITE

Next, write 1 John 2:7-9 in your "Write!" section.

READ

Please read Chapter 2 of 1 John.

INVESTIGATIVE STUDY
STREETVIEW: CHAPTER 2

Apply!

After reading Chapter 2 three times this week, have you noticed how many times John repeated the phrases, "I write" and "I have written?" He repeats things to make sure you know what is important.

Today, we are going to underline every time John uses the word "write" (or any word with "write" in it!). We will circle the person he is talking to.

Listed below are all the verses in which you will find the word "write." Put a check in the box as you do each one.

☐ 1 John 2:1   ☐ 1 John 2:7   ☐ 1 John 2:8   ☐ 1 John 2:12

☐ 1 John 2:13   ☐ 1 John 2:14   ☐ 1 John 2:21   ☐ 1 John 2:26

John wrote special notes to the "children," "fathers," and "young men" in verses 12 through 14.

He uses special family words to show his love for the Christians. There is no doubt that even though he is showing fatherly love to his children in the faith, His words were inspired by God. They are just like God calling us family through John's writing. How wonderful to be a part of Jesus' family if we call Him our Savior!

APPLY!

Families are so special! On a separate piece of paper, create a Family Tree. Be creative! You could use actual photos to place next to your family members' names or make your tree on a poster board. Interview a grandparent and put a short paragraph of a special story next to each person's name.

A.C.T.S. PRAYER TIME

"Before the mountains were brought forth, Or ever You had formed the earth and the world, even from everlasting to everlasting, You are God."
Psalm 90:2 New King James Version

A (Adoration)
"Dear Lord, You are..._____"

C (Confession)
"I am sorry for..._____"

T (Thanksgiving)
"Thank You for..._____"

S (Supplication)
"Please help me..._____"

D A Y   F O U R

ON MY KNEES:

Whoa! Are you in a hurry? S-L-O-W down and pause to pray. Share your heart with Jesus.

PRAY

"Lord, I feel like I want to hurry. I don't want to rush through our time. I want to show You that our time is most important. In Jesus' name, I pray, amen."

WRITE

Open your Bible to 1 John 2:10-13 and to write the verses in the "Write!" section of your Sword Study.

READ

Please read 1 John 2 before you begin your study time.

INVESTIGATIVE STUDY
STREETVIEW: CHAPTER 2

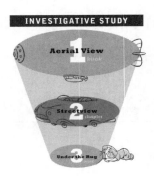

Apply!

Today we will be doing a treasure hunt. Hidden in 1 John 2 are some "if – then" statements. Some of them may be hard to find. Grab a sibling, friend or parent to do this together!

Scan the verses listed below looking for the word "if," then fill in the blanks below.

1. Verse 1:

If: _____ Then: _____

2. Verse 3:

If: _____ Then: _____

3. Verse 4:

If: _____ But:_____

Then:_____ And:_____

4. Verse 15:

If: _____ Then:_____

5. Verse 24:

If: _____ Then:_____

And:_____

6. Verse 29:

If: _____ Then:_____

A.C.T.S. Prayer Time

"My son, keep my words, and lay up my commandments with thee. Keep my commandments, and live; and my law as the apple of thine eye." Proverbs 7:1-2 King James Version

A (Adoration)
"Dear Lord, You are..._____"

C (Confession)
"I am sorry for..._____"

T (Thanksgiving)
"Thank You for..._____"

S (Supplication)
"Please help me..._____"

DAY FIVE

ON MY KNEES:

The weeks are flying by! Be encouraged faithful student of the Word. Begin your time in the Word with prayer.

PRAY

"Master, Savior, Lord of my heart, I come to you today to hear more teaching from the words of John. Open my ears to hear the things You want me to do. Train me through Your Bible. In Jesus' name, I pray, amen."

WRITE

As you write 1 John 2:14-16 behind the "Write!" tab of your Sword Study today, think about the words. Think about what the Word enables us to overcome.

READ

Wait! Don't open your Bible yet…move on to the INVESTIGATIVE STUDY section.

INVESTIGATIVE STUDY
STREETVIEW: CHAPTER 2

Apply!

We have three little projects we are going to do today.

First, John gives three exhortations to his readers. An exhortation is a command to act. The easiest way to find an exhortation is to search for a verb (the action word). We have given you the verses to look for in Chapter 2; you write the verb and the command that John writes in the verse.

1. Verse 15: Verb: _____

Command:_____

2. Verse 24: Verb: _____

Command:_____

3. Verse 28: Verb: _____

Command:_____

Now that you have done project number one, let's move to project number two! John gives us a list to describe the "world" in verses 16 and 17. On the lines below, write how he describes the world.

_____

_____

_____

_____

We want to make sure that you understand from the list that the world isn't the earth or people, it is the things in it. The things we want (toys, phones and money). John lists these things by saying that our flesh and eyes want them and they become the pride of our lives. The big word for this is materialism. Materialism wants stuff. Maybe you have heard of "stuff-mart"?

Next, trace the definitions below with a red colored pencil for two of the unique words that John used in 1 John 2.

Advocate:
<u>A person who defends or pleads for another's case</u>

(Example: My brother was an **advocate** for me when my dad thought that I was the one who broke the bike.)

Propitiation:

A payment _____

(Example: When I broke Mrs. Morris' window, my mom said that I owed a **propitiation** to make things right.)

A.C.T.S. Prayer Time

"Do not store up for yourselves treasures on earth, where moth and rust destroy, and where thieves break in and steal."
Matthew 6:19 New American Standard Version

A (Adoration)
"Dear Lord, You are..._____"

C (Confession)
"I am sorry for..._____"

T (Thanksgiving)
"Thank You for..._____"

S (Supplication)
"Please help me..._____"

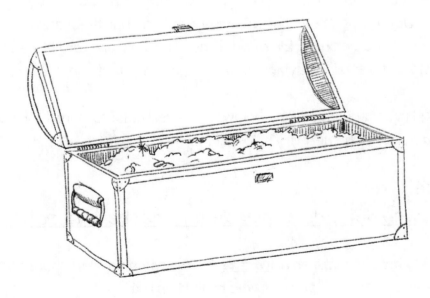

Samuel Morris: Light out of the Jungle
(Conclusion of speech given at Taylor University Convocation, September 9, 1892)

Some may find my story hard to believe. But some months later in a city near the coast of Africa, I met a boy who belonged to the enemy tribe. This young man had been present at the time of my capture and escape. "We did not know what had happened," he told me. "A bright light flashed over you. We heard someone call your name, and then you disappeared." After I explained the miracle, he decided to follow Christ, too.

Eager to learn more about God, I still had many questions. I decided to travel to America to expand my knowledge. I searched along the eastern African coast until I found a ship bound for America, but the captain refused to take me aboard. I begged God to change his heart. How could I have been surprised when He did?

Although I didn't know anything about ships, I was hired to take the place of a sailor who had fallen ill. The captain and his sailors drank too much and often treated me terribly. They beat me and assigned me the most difficult tasks. One tried to kill me. But I kept showing them the love of God, and before we landed on the shores of America, many of them—including the captain—had trusted Christ as their Savior.

When we arrived in New York City, I spent many months with Stephen Merritt, a man my missionary friend in Africa had said could teach me more. Stephen, a pastor, ran a homeless mission, and my desire to know God helped stir the hearts of the men there. Many became Christians.

As I spent time studying the Scriptures with Stephen, I found myself growing in the knowledge of God, right in line with my prayers. "You're moving from head knowledge (what you can know by sight and perception) to heart knowledge," Stephen said. "That's something you understand only by faith, deep within your spirit."

Along with the men of the homeless shelter, I was learning to abide in Christ, to remain with Him. This meant He had the freedom to rearrange any part of my life or character. I was not the same man I was back in Africa, nor was I the same man who landed in America. The Lord was growing and shaping me. I knew and believed the love He had for me (1 John 4:16). And without Him, I could do nothing.

Still, I wanted to know God more. "Go to Taylor University," Stephen urged. Dean Thaddeus Reade wanted me to come, too. In fact, he started an account to pay for my education that became known as the Samuel Faith Fund.

In December of 1891, I arrived here in Fort Wayne. When Dean Reade asked me which room I wanted, I told him the truth: "If there is a room nobody wants, give that to me."

I spent most of my evenings in that room talking to my Father, which most of you would call praying. Since I came to know Christ in that deeper way, it all seemed so simple. Like the apostle Paul, the great desire of my heart was to know Him more.

God used this desire to touch and transform the lives of the people who surrounded me. Local churches often invited me, their "missionary in ebony," to speak. I felt honored to share my story and was surprised when a local newspaper covered an all-night prayer service we held. It included the story of my capture and conversion, so almost everyone in the area grew to recognize the name Samuel Morris.

Likewise, the "Samuel Faith Fund" continued to grow as more and more donations came in. Soon, it held so much that Dean Reade could use it to help other needy students, too. A spiritual revival began in the town.

And that is where we find ourselves today. We are, as a town, a community and a college, longing to know Him more. We don't want to stay content with head-knowledge. We want to go beyond the facts.

Will you seek Him with me? Will you know and believe the love He has for you? I will be glad to speak with you in private, because I know He is longing to know you more.

Postscript: On May 12, 1893, Samuel Morris died after contracting a severe cold. His body never grew accustomed to the temperatures in America. But his death inspired many of his fellow students to serve as missionaries to Africa and fulfill his dream of one day returning to minister to his people. Today, Taylor University is still sending out missionaries, thanks more than a little to the life of a man of faith named Samuel Morris.

DAY ONE

ON MY KNEES:

Getting concerned with things in our lives can happen pretty easily. Our belongings can begin to rule us. The things of the world will pass away. John is going to tell us to focus on the things that will last, but first let's go to God in prayer.

PRAY

"Lord, lots of things are calling for my attention. I want to focus on You and Your Word now. Please drown out the noise so that I can concentrate on Your Word."

WRITE

As you write 1 John 2:17-19 in your copy of 1 John, highlight what lives forever in verse 17.

READ

STOP! Don't read anything yet. Go directly to the INVESTIGATIVE STUDY section.

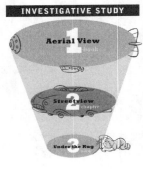

Apply!

INVESTIGATIVE STUDY STREETVIEW: CHAPTER 2

Grab your colored pencils. Skim through the second chapter of 1 John. Look for repeating words. Mark each word that you feel is important. Make up your own symbols, but be sure to mark all the references to God using the symbols we showed you earlier.

Today, we are going to get down into the words of 1 John 2. We are going UNDER THE RUG! Did you mark the word **know**?

The Greek words for **know** (**eido** and **ginosko**) are used over 30 times in John's small letter. This is why we chose to do our word study on these words.

Even though we use the same word in English, it can mean two different things. Read the two sentences below.

"Ashley **knows** the President because she <u>saw</u> his picture in the newspaper."
"Hunter **knows** the President because he <u>**personally**</u> worked with him for 10 years."

Who **knows** the President best? You are right, Hunter really **knows** the President. The word **know** can mean a common knowledge like when Jesus said that even the demons **know** God. He was saying that the demons had a common knowledge of God.

The other way the word **know** is used is to say that someone has a deep knowledge. Jesus said that those who **know** Him will love Him. John used different Greek words to make sure we **knew** what he meant. We can't tell which one John used in English, but we can when we look at the Greek! Read through the Word Studies of **know**. Then, we will investigate how John used the words.

PART A: When we looked up the word **know** in Strong's Concordance their numbers were 1492 and 1097. Below are the English words, the pronunciations, and the simple definitions from Strong's dictionary of the Greek words:

> **1492. Know,** <u>eido</u>. I'-do, a primary verb; to see.
> **1097. Know,** <u>ginosko</u>. ghin-oce-ko, verb; to understand, to be sure.

PART B: Next, if you look up the numbers 1492 and 1097 in another Greek dictionary, you can discover more detailed explanations of the word.

1492. Know:
    1. to see
        a. An acquaintance

1097. Know:
    1. To know deeply
        a. actively seeking to be good friends

PART C: Hang in there! We are not going to look at ALL 30 times that John uses the word **know**! We are just going to look at the ones in Chapter 2 since that is what we are studying.

First, there is one verse in 1 John 2 that uses both of our Greek words for **know.**

"If ye **know** (1492) that he is righteous, ye **know** (1097) that every one that doeth righteousness is born of God" 1 John 2:29

Next, let's take a look at the verses that used 1492. This is the common knowledge word for **know**. With your Bible open to Chapter 2, find the verse below and put the letter "S" or the word "See" above the word "**know**" or in the margin of your Bible. This will remind you of which Greek word for **know** is being used whenever you read the verses!

1 John 2:11
1 John 2:20
1 John 2:21 (both instances)

Now, do the same exercise with the verses that used 1097 meaning deep knowledge or understanding. Insert the letter "D" (for DEEPLY **know**) before the word **know** in each of the following passages.

1 John 2:3 (both instances)
1 John 2:4
1 John 2:18
1 John 2:29

In summary, we can **know** (1097) someone really well if we spend time with them. We get to **know** Jesus by studying His Word.

APPLY!

Is there a new family at your church? Ask your parents if they could come for lunch after church or if you can call one of the children that are close to your age. Welcome them and ask if you could interview them to get to know them better. Plan ahead with a parent by coming up with your interview questions before you call!

A.C.T.S. PRAYER TIME

"but lay up for yourselves treasures in heaven, where neither moth nor rust destroys and where thieves do not break in and steal. For where your treasure is, there your heart will be also." Matthew 6:20-21 English Standard Version

A (Adoration)

"Dear Lord, You are..._____"

C (Confession)

"I am sorry for..._____"

T (Thanksgiving)

"Thank You for..._____"

S (Supplication)

"Please help me..._____"

DAY TWO

ON MY KNEES:

A new day has arrived. You will have many choices today. God is pleased that you chose to spend time with Him. God tells us to seek Him.

PRAY

"Heavenly Father, I want to know You much better than I do now. Help me to press on in today's study. Wake my heart up! In Jesus' name, I pray."

WRITE

Please open up to the "Write!" section of your Sword Study. Today, let's write 1 John 2:20-23.

READ

Today, read both Chapters 1 and 2 of 1 John.

INVESTIGATIVE STUDY
UNDER THE RUG: CROSS REFERENCES - "KNOW"

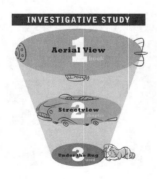

Apply!

One of the main reasons God gave us the Bible is so that we could really **know** Him. The Bible tells us the way to fellowship with God forever. Today, we are going to look at the word **know**, with a capital "D" for DEEPLY **know** in other verses. Are you ready? GO!

Look up and read Psalm 36:7-10*.

Who receives lovingkindness/love? (v. 7)_____

Where do they see the light? (v. 9)_____

Who receives God's lovingkindness/love? (v. 10)_____

Look up and read Hosea 6:3-6*.

What is the command in verse 3?_____

What does God want from us? (v. 6)_____

What happens when we *know* God? (v. 3)_____

Look up and read John 8:31-32*.

Who are Jesus' disciples?_____

What do His disciples *know?*_____

What does this knowledge do for the disciple?_____

Look up and read John 17:3*.

What is eternal life?_____

_____

A.C.T.S. Prayer Time

"I have not departed from the commandment of His lips; I have treasured the words of His mouth more than my necessary food." Job 23:12 New King James Version

A (Adoration)
"Dear Lord, You are..._____"

C (Confession)
"I am sorry for..._____"

T (Thanksgiving)
"Thank You for..._____"

S (Supplication)
"Please help me..._____"

DAY THREE

ON MY KNEES:

Sit down. Relax. You are starting your day in a great way! Coming to the Lord for His wisdom is what will make you strong. We just can't live right without Him. Begin with prayer.

PRAY

"Lord, I want to really know You. Shed light on the passages I am about to study so I can understand them. Amen."

WRITE

Turn to the "Write!" section of your study and copy 1 John 2:24-26 on the page.

READ

Find a sibling. Call a grandparent. Dial a friend. Read 1 John 2 together. Make the time short. Read and pray and then carry on with your study.

INVESTIGATIVE STUDY
UNDER THE RUG: WORD STUDY - "ABIDE"

Apply!

We are going to study the word **abide** next. John uses this word over and over in Chapter 2. We have been marking it with little feet. Maybe you will be able to guess why after you study its Greek word! Read on to find out more.

<u>PART A:</u> If you were to look up the word **abide** in Strong's Concordance, you would find that the Strong's number assigned to it in 1 John is number 3306. Below is the word written in English, the pronunciation, and the basic definition from the Strong's dictionary.

3306. Abide. <u>menō.</u> *men-o,* a verb; to stay in a given place: continue, dwell, endure, be present, remain, stand, tarry.

<u>Part B</u>
1) to remain, dwell, live
   a. In a place
   b. One person remains with another person in heart, mind and will.

<u>Part C</u>: John uses the word **abide** to describe a person who remains with another person. When he uses this word, he means that we are sticking with them with all of our heart, mind and will. We are walking with them, like them and for them! Does this remind you of little walking feet? ☺

John uses this word all over 1 John, but we are only going to question the verses in Chapter 2. Look at the verses that have the word **abide** in them. Answer the question next to each reference.

According to verse 6, what should the person who **abides** in God be doing?

_____

Who **abides** in the light, according to verse 10?_____

Where does the Word of God **abide**, according to verse 14?_____

In verse 17, what **abides** forever?_____

With whom do we **abide**, according to verse 24?_____

According to verse 27, where do we **abide**?_____

Who is supposed to **abide** in God, according to verse 28?_____

Remaining...or sticking with the Lord and His ways is how we "walk" through life as a Christian. If you have the time and energy, mark the word **abide** in your Bible with little feet before closing in prayer.

A.C.T.S. Prayer Time

"For the Lord gives wisdom; from His mouth come knowledge and understanding; He stores up sound wisdom for the upright; He is a shield to those who walk uprightly;"
Proverbs 2:6-7 New King James Version

A (Adoration)

"Dear Lord, You are..._____"

C (Confession)

"I am sorry for..._____"

T (Thanksgiving)

"Thank You for..._____"

S (Supplication)

"Please help me..._____"

D A Y   F O U R

ON MY KNEES:

Sometimes we are tired or don't feel like we have the strength to live for Jesus. We need to go to Him, tell Him how we are feeling and ask Him for strength. Let's do that now.

PRAY

"You are my Rock and my mighty Fortress, Lord. I am asking for Your strength for myself and those who are studying Your Word with me. Help us to not give up fellowshipping with You. In Your powerful name, I pray, amen."

WRITE

As you write 1 John 2:27-29, stop and read John's words out loud.

READ

As we near the end of our study of 1 John, Chapter 2, remember the reason we study the Bible is to know Jesus! Read 1 John 2.

INVESTIGATIVE STUDY
UNDER THE RUG: CROSS REFERENCES - "ABIDE"

Apply!

Being on the same team can be fun. Teamwork is a good example of **abiding** with people who have the same purpose.

Come on, we are going to explore more passages to expand our understanding of the word **abide**.

Read Psalm 15:1-5.

Wow! List all of the characteristics of those who **abide** with the Lord.

_____   _____

_____   _____

_____   _____

_____   _____

_____   _____

_____

Why don't we have to **abide** (remain) in darkness, according to John 12:46?

_____

Who did Jesus give us that **abides** with us, according to John 14:16-17?

_____

A.C.T.S. Prayer Time

"The LORD is my strength and my song, and he has become my salvation; this is my God, and I will praise him, my father's God, and I will exalt him." - Exodus 15:2 NASB

A (Adoration)
"Dear Lord, You are..._____"

C (Confession)
"I am sorry for..._____"

T (Thanksgiving)
"Thank You for..._____"

S (Supplication)
"Please help me..._____"

Digging Deeper!

Read what Jesus says in John 15:5. Then, answer the questions below.

Who is the vine?_____

Who are the branches?_____

What happens when we **abide** with the vine?_____

What happens when we do not **abide** with the vine?_____

DAY FIVE

ON MY KNEES:

We are finishing up another week of 1 John. We are done with Chapter 2! How wonderful and excellent is the Word of God. Here we find God stories, answers to our questions and, most importantly, God's love for us. We find Jesus as our way to have an eternal relationship with His Father, God. Let's pray before we do our Day 10 Diagram.

PRAY

"How excellent is Your name! You are Holy and I am not. Help me to abide in Your light today. I don't want to go off the path to the left or to the right. Light my day with Your words and gentle training. Amen."

WRITE

Take time to look over your handwirtten copy of 1 John 2. Have you marked all the references to God with your symbols? If not, do so now.

READ

Quietly read 1 John, Chapter 2.

1-2-3 SUMMARIZE: CHAPTER 2

Apply!

Have you been looking forward to doing the Diagram throughout the week? Remember, if you have any issues figuring out how to fill in your Day 10 Diagram, talk to a parent; their Guidebook includes a key to this diagram.

☐ To begin, look at the top of the Day 10 Diagram. Fill in the chapter number. Look at Week 1, Day 5 for the original title you created for 1 John 2. Review what you wrote and refine your title with the new insights that you have learned over the last 10 days.

☐ Next, which verse from the chapter do you think was the "key verse?"

☐ On the right of the page, transfer your key Greek words from this chapter. Write the English words on the top line after the words "Greek Words." Transfer the Greek spellings and write a short definition of their meanings.

☐ On the bottom of the Diagram page, transfer the most important things that you learned about God through marking the references about Him on your "Write!" pages.

Let's continue walking along with John and our fellow travelers as we fill in this next

Day 10 Diagram. In Chapter 2, John identified the recipients of his letter and gave his reasons for writing to them. Underneath each person in the diagram, label one of the three groups to which John was writing. Then, on the blanks to the right of John and the young Christians, list John's stated reasons for writing to that group. Finally, on the left of each person, label the appropriate description that John says should characterize that group of recipients. (Hints: John is carrying a Bible, the young man has a walking stick, and the young lady has a heart next to her feet.)

If John's recipients (and we) are faithful to God's exhortations in John's letter, then we will not be captured in the destructive trap of loving the world. In the center of the circle that represents the world system, write "The World" under the crossed-out heart. In the other four blanks within the circle, list the attributes that John notes about the world in 1 John 2:16-17.

Above the deceptive lure of the world system, the cross stands strong and true. In Chapter 2, John said that Jesus is our _____ when we sin; write this title for Jesus at the top of the cross. At the shining foot of the cross, note once again that "God is Light." How good it is to know that we have been freed from the world and can walk in the light with God!

A.C.T.S. Prayer Time

"But the path of the righteous is like the light of dawn, that shines brighter and brighter until the full day." Proverbs 4:18 New American Standard Bible

A (Adoration)

"Dear Lord, You are..._____"

C (Confession)

"I am sorry for..._____"

T (Thanksgiving)

"Thank You for..._____"

S (Supplication)

"Please help me..._____"

Title: _____

Chapter: ___:___

Key Verse: _____

Greek Words: _____

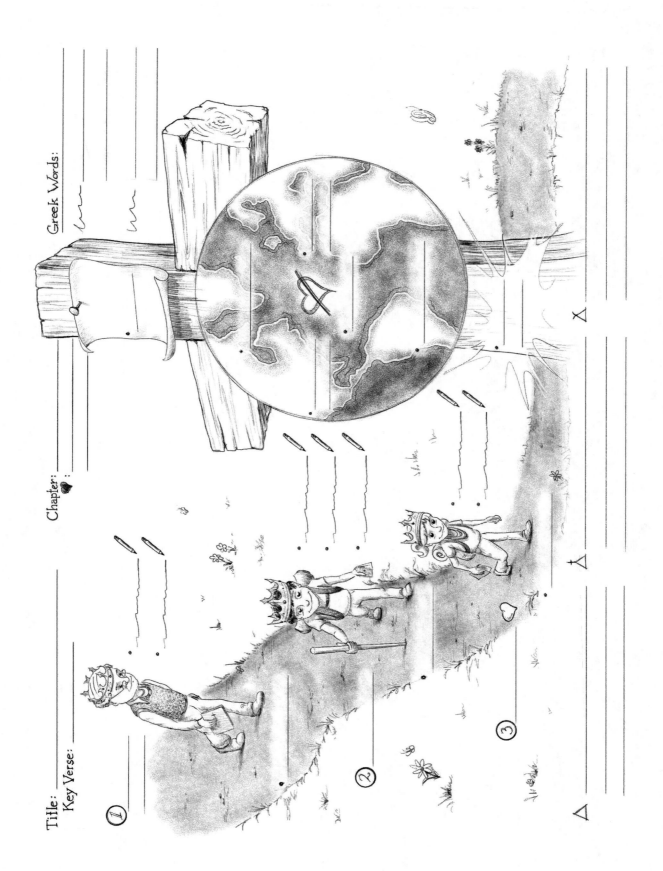

109

Billy Graham: Light to the Nations

November 1, 1934

I don't keep up with my journal as often as I should, but I wanted to be sure and record something today. Today, this old (I'll be sixteen in a few days) farm boy from Charlotte, North Carolina made a decision that will change my life forever: I received Christ as my Lord and Savior. Instead of calling religion "hogwash," as I did not long ago, I'm a child of God!

What does that mean? At this point, I'm not exactly sure—at least not in terms of how it affects my daily life. I do know that our visiting preacher, Mordecai Ham, explained the beauty of heaven and the reality of hell. He told us if we died without accepting Christ's death on the cross as the substitute for our sin, we'd end up separated from God forever.

I've always thought the Bible was true. I just never thought it applied to me. But tonight when Rev. Ham explained, it all seemed crystal-clear. It made the hours I've spent in the hayloft reading books seem nothing more than a waste of time. This one book, this precious old Book, is the one that matters most.

I received Jesus today, and I know my life will never be the same.

February 15, 1939

Today marked another milestone in my walk with Christ. That's because the St. John's River Council (a group of Baptist pastors) here in Tampa, Florida ordained me. Now, I'm set apart as a minister of the gospel, commissioned to spread His light.

More than two years ago, I first sensed the Lord calling me to preach. Like Moses, I fought it, thinking up all kinds of excuses. But God persisted. One night more than a year ago, as I walked the eighteenth green of the Temple Terrace Golf Course, the Holy Spirit overtook me. I dropped to my knees and cried, "Oh God, if You want me to preach, I will serve You."

The council asked many questions about what I believe and why. It was a good thing I had my answers all ready, because I was too nervous to think and just blurted out whatever came to mind. But those answers must have been pretty close to right, because the council approved me. I guess the good Lord was giving His child words to speak, just like the Scripture says.

I haven't written in my journal for some time. I stay so busy studying that I'm having a hard time keeping up. My school is called the Florida Bible Institute. Until this year, I was enrolled at Bob Jones University, but I feel so much more at home here.

My intention, unless God shows me otherwise, is to graduate from this fine institution and then head to Illinois and finish out my education at Wheaton College. Nothing can stop me now!

June 10, 1943

I'm just a few days away from receiving my degree in anthropology from Wheaton. To say the least, it's been an enlightening four years. And one of the biggest lights has been a young lady, Miss Ruth Bell. She and I intend to be married later this summer. What's so special about her?

Everything. Before I met her, I heard about her from a friend. He told me that besides being the most beautiful girl he'd ever met, she got up every morning at four to pray. She grew up as a missionary kid in China and has a heart for the lost.

A girl like that sounded too good for me, and too good to be true. But once I met her, I knew I wanted to see more of her.

On our first date, we went to see Handel's Messiah. And it didn't take long after that for both of us to realize God had a "Hallelujah" for us in each other. We don't know everything that lies ahead. But we do know we want to spend the rest of our days together. Thank You, Lord, for giving me Ruth. "He finds a wife finds a good thing and receives favor from the Lord" (Prov. 18:22).

December 5, 1949

My life seems to be changing once again. For a short time, I pastured a small Baptist church in Illinois. Ruth and I were happy there, but the Lord called us to a different kind of service.

I started traveling and leading meetings for Youth for Christ, an organization created to tell servicemen returning from the war and other young people about God. Before long, my fame as an evangelist started to spread. I wanted to see more people move from the kingdom of darkness to light, from living as children of the devil to new life as children of God. Along the way, I kept preaching at various churches, revival services and crusades.

Not long ago, a group, "Christ for Greater Los Angeles," invited me to preach at their Los Angeles crusade. God moved, and what started as a three-week revival continued for an additional five weeks. I know the Lord is moving me toward a life as an evangelist.

Still, I dread the publicity associated with these events. I've been preaching crusades for long enough to understand that you can't manufacture the Holy Spirit. He's the One who draws people to the Father. And He's the One who makes us His children.

Forever.

Enjoy more excerpts from Billy Graham's life and ministry next week!

DAY ONE

ON MY KNEES:

Hooray, we are at Chapter 3! Are you excited to see what God will show you in this chapter? Or, are you unsure if you feel like continuing? Turn to the Lord and share how you are feeling today.

PRAY

"All-knowing God and Father, even though You know my heart and thoughts, You ask me to come and share them with You. I want to be excited to sit at Your feet, yet I confess that at times it is hard to come when there are other things to do. Make this next chapter of 1 John speak to me personally. In Your precious name, I pray, amen."

WRITE

Grab a red pen or pencil so that you will have it nearby as you copy 1 John 3 into your "Write!" pages. Each time you write the word "love," use your red pen. You could draw a red heart around it, too. Begin with 1 John 3:1-2 today.

READ

Keep your Bible open and read 1 John 3.

INVESTIGATIVE STUDY
STREETVIEW: CHAPTER 3

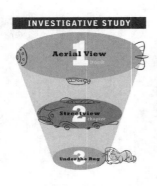

Apply!

Time to turn the tables! We would like you to write a question for some of the verses in Chapter 3. You read the verse and then write a question. Place a star next to your favorite question so you can share it at your Family Bonfire.

Verse 1: _____

Answer: _____

Verse 4: _____

Answer: _____

Verse 5: _____

Answer: _____

Verse 7: _____

Answer: _____

Verse 11: _____

Answer: _____

Good job! Now, grab one of your brothers, sisters or a parent and give them your quiz! Tomorrow, we will do a few more of Chapter 3's verses.

A.C.T.S. Prayer Time

"No soldier gets entangled in civilian pursuits, since his aim is to please the one who enlisted him." 2 Timothy 2:4 English Standard Version

A (Adoration)
"Dear Lord, You are..._____"

C (Confession)
"I am sorry for..._____"

T (Thanksgiving)
"Thank You for..._____"

S (Supplication)
"Please help me..._____"

DAY TWO

ON MY KNEES:

Do you have a favorite song that you sing at church? A Psalm is a song that worships God. Take the time before you begin to use a song as your prayer to Jesus.

PRAY

Write the name of the song you sang here: _____

WRITE

Now, write 1 John 3:3-4 on the next lines in your copy of 1 John.

READ

Quietly, but out loud, read 1 John 3 again.

INVESTIGATIVE STUDY
STREETVIEW: CHAPTER 3

Apply!

Did you notice how much you learned writing your own questions for each verse? You have to really read the verse and listen to what is being said to write a question.

When you are finished, maybe you could call a friend (the one you check in with weekly to stay accountable for your Sword Study) and share each other's questions!

Verse 13: _____

Answer: _____

Verse 15: _____

Answer: _____

Verse 17: _____

Answer: _____

Verse 18: _____

Answer: _____

Verse 23: _____

Answer: _____

Verse 24: _____

Answer: _____

A.C.T.S. Prayer Time

"Praise him with the timbrel and dance: praise him with stringed instruments and organs. Praise him upon the loud cymbals: praise him upon the high sounding cymbals. Let everything that hath breath praise the Lord. Praise ye the Lord."
Psalm 150:4-6 (KJV)

What talent or talents has the Lord given you to praise His name and worship Him? Can you play the piano? Cymbals? Take the time today to worship the Lord through song. If you don't play an instrument, simply put on a pair of earphones, turn on your favorite hymn or song of praise. Go to a quiet, out-of-way place and sing unto the Lord, then close in prayer using the verse above!

A (Adoration)
"Dear Lord, You are..._____"

C (Confession)
"I am sorry for..._____"

T (Thanksgiving)
"Thank You for..._____"

S (Supplication)
"Please help me..._____"

DAY THREE

ON MY KNEES:

The earth and everything in it gives proof of God. For example, when we look at an Okapi (Do you know what that is?) we can see how creative God is in His creation. What a blessing to know that God tells us more about Himself through His Word. Start your day by praising Him in prayer!

PRAY

"Creator and Master Artist, Your creations are wonderful, but You, Yourself, deserve praise. Thank You for giving me examples of Your presence everywhere I turn. From the creatures to scenery, I can witness Your greatness. Show me more about Yourself today. Amen."

WRITE

1 John 3:5-7 are your next verses to write in your "My Copy of 1 John."

READ

Take a moment, go outside with your Bible and read 1 John 3. Leave everything else in your special spot.

INVESTIGATIVE STUDY
STREETVIEW: CHAPTER 3

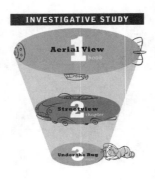

Apply!

As you questioned the 3rd chapter of 1 John, did you notice that John added a new comparison?

What two children are compared in 1 John 3:10?

Children/Sons of _____

and Children/Sons of _____

When he gave us the comparison, he also gives us a new reason to rejoice about our relationship with God. John reminds us that God loved us so much He has called us children of God! We have been adopted into the family of God. How amazing! How incredible! We are not just friends, we are a part the Royal family!

Today, we are going to look at the characteristics of the children of God and tomorrow, we will investigate the other family, the children of the devil.

What did God's love do, according to John 3:16?_____

Who can call themselves children of God, according to John 1:12?_____

_____

What are the children of God called in Ephesians 5:8?_____

Back to 1 John 3; verses 6 and 9 speak of practicing sin. Why don't the sons of God practice sin?_____

According to 1 John 3:10, what are two characteristics of the children of God?

_____

A.C.T.S. Prayer Time

"Every day will I bless thee; and I will praise thy name forever and ever. Great is the Lord, and greatly to be praised; and his greatness is unsearchable. The Lord is gracious, and full of compassion; slow to anger, and of great mercy. The Lord is good to all: and his tender mercies are over all his works. All thy works shall praise thee, O Lord; and thy saints shall bless thee."
Psalm 145:1-3, 8-10 King James Version

A (Adoration)
"Dear Lord, You are..._____"

C (Confession)
"I am sorry for..._____"

T (Thanksgiving)
"Thank You for..._____"

S (Supplication)
"Please help me..._____"

D A Y   F O U R

ON MY KNEES:

Did you get enough rest last night? Are you tired from all the activities on your schedule? God tells us to "come" and He "will give us rest" when we have worked hard living in His ways. Go to Him in prayer, for there you will find peace.

PRAY

"Lord, my life can seem too hard sometimes. Help me to learn more about You and trust You more, so that I rest in Your ways. In Your powerful name, I pray. Amen"

WRITE

Turn to 1 John 3 and write verses 8 through 10.

READ

Is there someone you can grab to read 1 John, Chapter 3 with you?

INVESTIGATIVE STUDY
STREETVIEW: CHAPTER 3

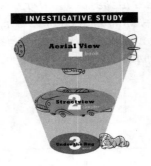

Apply!

Today, we will investigate the children of the devil. First, we will review John's descriptions in 1 John, then we will look for more information in other Scripture passages.

According to verse 4, what is another word that defines practicing sin?

_____

What was a reason Jesus came to earth, according to verse 8?

_____

What two things describe children of the devil? (verse 10)

_____   _____

Who is given as an example of the evil one in verse 12? _____

   We want to remember that if a person is not for God, then he is against God. Even though a person is a child of the devil, the children of God need to love him and share the Good News so that he can become a child of God.

   Just like 1 John 2:2 says, Jesus was everyone's payment for sin. We want the family of God to grow! Now, let's look at the devil and his sons in other Bible passages.

Who are the children of the devil worshipping in Matthew 4:9-10? _____

Read Acts 13:10 and answer the questions below.

What is the child of the devil full of? _____

What is the enemy of the child of the devil? _____

What does he do to the right ways of the Lord? _____

What do you learn about the devil in 1 Peter 5:8? _____

_____

   Children of God, rejoice! Our Father is the Beginning and the End, the One who will win...THE ALMIGHTY. There is none-- no, not anyone, that can defeat or destroy our heavenly Father. Go to Him in prayer, rejoicing all the way!

APPLY!

Just as 1 John 3:18 tells us to love in deed and truth, is there someone with whom you can share the Good News in word or action? Pray that God would bring someone to your mind to whom you can be an example of His love in how you talk or live. Write his or her name here, pray for him or her and be ready to share the Good News of Jesus if you are asked about why you live the way you do.

My friend's name:_____

A.C.T.S. PRAYER TIME

"Therefore, God has highly exalted him and bestowed on him the name that is above every name, so that at the name of Jesus every knee should bow, in heaven and on earth and under the earth, and every tongue confess that Jesus Christ is lord, to the glory of God the Father." Philippians 2: 9-11 English Standard Version

A (Adoration)

"Dear Lord, You are..._____"

C (Confession)

"I am sorry for..._____"

T (Thanksgiving)

"Thank You for..._____"

S (Supplication)

"Please help me..._____"

DAY FIVE

ON MY KNEES:

We are halfway through our study of 1 John! HOORAY for you! You have been a faithful student of the Word! Let's thank the Lord for the strength He has given us.

PRAY

"Lord, You are strong. You are the Strongest. When I am tired and feel like giving up, help me to depend on Your strength. I know You want me to seek You in the Scriptures. Help me finish the race of studying 1 John. In Your strong name, I pray. Amen."

WRITE

I John 3:11-12

READ

Turn to Genesis, Chapter 4 and read verses 1-16. Yes, **Genesis** 4:1-16.

INVESTIGATIVE STUDY STREETVIEW: CHAPTER 3

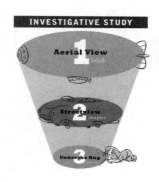

Apply!

Today, we are going to take a short break from the book of 1 John. Since John mentioned the example of Cain to his audience, it is important for us to go back and look what happened with the first family.

Use Genesis 4:1-16 to answer the questions below

Aerial View of Cain's Example...

Who were Cain's parents? _____

Who was Cain's brother? _____

What was Cain's job? _____

What was Abel's job? _____

STREETVIEW of Cain's Example...

Did Cain know what offering the Lord expected from him? _____

What did Cain do to Abel? _____

What was Cain's punishment? _____

_____

UNDER THE RUG View of Cain's Example (in Cross Reference Passages)...

According to Matthew 23:35, was Abel guilty of any sin against Cain? _____

Whose blood is mentioned in Hebrews 12:24 that speaks better than Abel's blood?
_____

Jumping back to 1 John 3:12...

Why was he called a son of the evil one? _____

What was said about Abel? _____

A.C.T.S. Prayer Time

"For the Lord God is a sun and shield; The Lord will give grace and glory; No good thing will He withhold from those who walk uprightly."

Psalm 84:11 New King James Version

A (Adoration)

"_____"

C (Confession)

"_____"

T (Thanksgiving)

"_____"

S (Supplication)

"_____"

Digging Deeper!

Find a quiet time this weekend and re-read the whole book of 1 John.

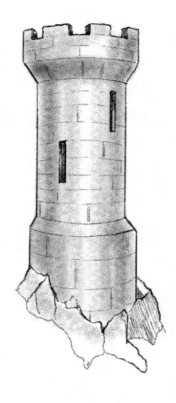

Billy Graham: Light to the Nations

By 1950, Billy's ministry had expanded so much that he, his wife, and some associates (evangelist Grady Wilson, master of ceremonies Cliff Burrows, soloist George Beverly Shea and Youth for Christ coworker George Wilson) organized the Billy Graham Evangelistic Association (BGEA). Its purpose was to help run Billy's ministry in an orderly, business-like manner.

The BGEA planned and coordinated meetings and crusades for Graham and his associate evangelists. It also owned Graham's weekly radio program, The Hour of Decision. As it expanded, the BGEA started a popular magazine, Decision, along with a division that produced evangelistic films. Many of these films featured actual footage from the Billy Graham crusades.

Let's read some of the stories of those whose lives have been touched and changed through the ministry of the BGEA. Although the stories are true, names and identifying details have been changed.

Norman: I can hardly wait to read Dr. Graham's latest book. As a San Francisco teenager, I gave my life to Christ at his big Crusade there. Today, I'm still going strong in the Lord. He has protected me through hearts attacks and strokes, and I will always love Him. May He continue to be with you, Billy.

Darlene: Billy, you've been an inspiration to me throughout my Christian life. I came to know Jesus during one of your Canadian Crusades in 1974. Today, I watch your sermons on television and in person, too. I have never for one second regretted turning my life over to my Lord and Savior, Jesus Christ. Thank you for taking His message to the world!

Pete: I accepted Jesus Christ as my Savior during a crusade at Memorial Coliseum in 1965. I played high school football there and remember the event as if it were yesterday. My knees rested on the thirty-yard line when Christ entered my life.

I'm so grateful to Billy for sharing Christ with me. Now nearly sixty, I was sixteen at the time I got saved and have been serving the Lord ever since. Following Christ was the most important decision I ever made. God bless you, Billy, for touching my life.

Renee: I was a privileged teenager who grew up in Sacramento, California. In the late 1950s, I sang in the choir at the Billy Graham Crusade there and was preparing to leave as a short-term missionary in Africa.

At the same time, I had a heavy heart. I didn't know whether or not either of my parents had a genuine relationship with the Lord. I found myself praying for them constantly.

Several years later, while serving in Africa, I wrote my parents to ask if they knew Christ. I was amazed at the answer. Without my realizing it, my parents had attended the Crusade when I sang in the choir. They had both gone forward to receive Christ at Dr. Graham's invitation.

Thank you, Billy Graham, for proclaiming the message of salvation in such a clear manner. Because of you, I'll see my parents in heaven one day.

Clifford: Dr. Billy Graham and his ministry have changed my life. In the early 1980s, I was involved in a religious cult. But I watched a Billy Graham crusade on television and was born again. I thank God for using Dr. Graham to bring me out of the darkness and into the light of His love.

Susan: I had always been a religious person, someone who attended church all my life. But inside, I was empty.

I went with my church group to Explo '72 in Dallas, Texas. Bill Bright and Billy Graham shared the gospel with us, and I remember coming forward to confirm my faith. After that meeting and prayer, I knew with confidence that Jesus Christ had come into my heart as my Lord and Savior.

I praise God for Billy Graham. He stepped across denominational lines to proclaim the truth. He has brought unity to the body of Christ and is a model for every minister who shares the gospel today. He leads his ministry with purity of heart and integrity, both of which are rare these days. He is the kind of righteous man Scripture praises, for his righteousness comes from God. May the Lord bless you, Billy Graham!

Johnny: I grew up in Charleston, South Carolina, and I can hardly remember a Sunday morning or evening that our family wasn't worshiping at our local church.

I was the youngest of four children. Since my siblings participated in all sorts of church activities, I did, too: Vacation Bible School, retreats, youth choir and retreats throughout the year. I had a happy childhood and was a "good boy." I knew a lot about the Bible, but I had never made a public decision for Christ.

But in 1968, when I was fourteen years old, our church youth group went to see a BGEA movie called *For Pete's Sake*. Through watching the movie, I realized I could never be "good." Through the movie, I heard and responded to a Billy Graham invitation to accept Christ. I wrote the date on the back of my ticket stub with a reminder of my decision. Although I grew up in the Church, God used a man named Billy Graham and his World Wide Pictures to save my soul for eternity.

Praise God for how He used this faithful servant in so many lives around the world! Billy Graham is mostly retired at 94 years of age, now, but the BGEA continues to influence countless lives for Christ.

D A Y   O N E

ON MY KNEES:

Did you have a good weekend? Did you enjoy being at your church? We hope you heard a great message from God's Word and enjoyed fellowship with other children of God. Let's pray.

PRAY

"Lord, thank You for giving me friends and family who love You. Help me to be like a tree planted by water which grows a lot of fruit. Encourage me through the words of 1 John."

WRITE

Turn to your "Write" pages and write I John 3:13-15.

READ

When you read 1 John 3 today, watch for words that you think would be good Key Words.

INVESTIGATIVE STUDY
UNDER THE RUG: WORD STUDY -
"RIGHTEOUS"

Apply!

Now that you have read through Chapter 3 six times, do you have any Key Words you want to investigate?

We have chosen **righteous** and **righteousness**. You may not have picked either of these words as there are only three times John uses them in Chapter 3. Sometimes a Key Word is used a couple of times in each chapter, and by the time the author is finished, the word has become a theme word. This is why we chose **righteous** and **righteousness**. You will see this as we do our word studies. For now, let's begin looking at the word **righteous**.

PART A: If you were to look up the word **righteous** in Strong's Concordance, you would find that the Strong's number assigned to it in 1 John is 1342. Below is the word written in English, the pronunciation, and the basic definition from the Strong's dictionary.

1342. Righteous. <u>dikaios.</u> dik-ah-yos; from 1349: holy, just, right.

PART B:

1) That which is right.
    a. God is the creator of the rules and regulations that man must live by in order to be called righteous.
    b. A person who acts according to God's rules.
    c. God is the only person who never fails.

    A **righteous** person lives according to God's rules instead of their own rules. The Bible tells us that we need to hear what God wants and live like He wants us to live. All of the passages below give us examples of what this means to us.

Turn to Matthew 5:43-45 and answer the questions below:

What is man's rule? _____

What is God's rule? _____

According to Matthew 25:35-40, what are some of "God's expected ways of behavior" for the **righteous** man? _____

_____

How is **righteous** described in Luke 1:6? _____

_____

How are the *righteous* to live, according to Romans 1:17? _____

_____

Note all that you learn about the *righteous* in 1 Peter 3:8-12 on the lines below:

_____

_____

_____

A.C.T.S. Prayer Time

"Behold, I am the LORD, the God of all flesh: is there anything too hard for me?"
- Jeremiah 32:27 King James Version

A (Adoration)
"Dear Lord, You are..._____"

C (Confession)
"I am sorry for..._____"

T (Thanksgiving)
"Thank You for..._____"

S (Supplication)
"Please help me..._____"

DAY TWO

ON MY KNEES:

Sometimes we are more concerned about looking "right" in front of our friends than how we look before God. Let's go to the Most Righteous of all in prayer.

PRAY

"Righteous God, You are just and good all the time. Help me to live in a way that shows I am in Your family. I want to be a doer of the Word, not just a hearer. Show me how today. Amen."

WRITE

When you write 1 John 3:16-18, watch for the direction John gives to the children.

READ

Read 1 John 3 from start to finish.

INVESTIGATIVE STUDY
UNDER THE RUG: WORD STUDY -
"RIGHTEOUSNESS"

Apply!

"You know, I am pretty good." "I'm really nice to all of my friends." "Really, compared to so-and-so, I am nearly perfect." Ooh, how easy it can be to compare ourselves to one another. Let's look at the Greek word that John used for **righteousness** to see where we should be looking for comparisons.

PART A: If you were to look up the word **righteousness** in Strong's Concordance, you would find that the Strong's number assigned to it in 1 John 3:7 is 1343. Below is the way the word is written in English, the pronunciation, and the basic definition from the Strong's dictionary.

1343. Righteousness. <u>dikaiosunē,</u> dik-ah-yos-oo-nay; from 1342: equity, justification.

<u>Part B</u>

1) Conforming to God's law
2) Opposite of lawlessness and sin
3) The deeds or doing of right

Part C: John was telling all the children of God that they needed to do what was right. If they were really God's children then they had to live what was right in God's eye. If we say we believe and know God, then our lives have to match the words our tongues say.

The **righteous** are busy doing what is right. They are busy at **righteousness**! The passages below give an example of doing right... or being unrighteous. If the verse is an example of doing right, circle Right. If the reference is an example of doing wrong, circle Wrong.

1 John 1:6   Right   or   Wrong

Note to Myself: _____

1 John 2:4   Right   or   Wrong

Note to Myself: _____

1 John 2:21   Right   or   Wrong

Note to Myself: _____

1 John 3:7   Right   or   Wrong

Note to Myself: _____

1 John 3:12   Right   or   Wrong

Note to Myself: _____

    Children of God, pray that the Lord will help you walk in a **righteous** way as you finish your time in God's Word today.

APPLY!

    Grab a few siblings or friends and play a new board game. Wait! First, read the rules. Then, make one person a judge. Whenever there is a question about how the game is played, the judge is responsible to refer to the rules and make sure the game is being played righteously!

A.C.T.S. PRAYER TIME

"For the Lord gives wisdom; from His mouth come knowledge and understanding; He stores up sound wisdom for the upright; He is a shield to those who walk uprightly;"
- Proverbs 2:6-7 New King James Version

A (Adoration)
"Dear Lord, You are..._____"

C (Confession)
"I am sorry for..._____"

T (Thanksgiving)
"Thank You for..._____"

S (Supplication)
"Please help me..._____"

Day Three

On My Knees:

We are God's little children if we have believed in Jesus' name for our salvation. Bow before your Heavenly Father in prayer before we go to the study of His Word.

PRAY

"Father, yes Heavenly Father, I am honored to be one of Your children. I know that through Your Word that I am Yours. Continue to give me confidence in Your love. Amen."

WRITE

Write 1 John 3:19-21 on the next lines of your "My Copy of 1 John" pages.

READ

Read 1 John 3 aloud.

INVESTIGATIVE STUDY
UNDER THE RUG: CROSS REFERENCES - "RIGHTEOUS"

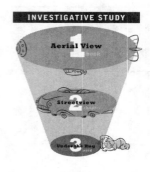

Apply!

Today, we are going to take a slight turn from our normal cross reference verses. We will still look at Scripture containing the word **righteous**, but we are going to look at people who were called **righteous**.

We can learn from their examples since God said they lived a **righteous** life. We will give you a passage. You write in the name of the **righteous** person and then say what he did that was **righteous**. (If you are using the King James Version, the word "just" is sometimes used for **righteous**.)

Read Genesis 6:5-9.

Person: _____

Summary: _____

_____

Read Luke 2:25.

Person: _____

Summary: _____

_____

Read Luke 23:50-53.

Person: _____

Summary: _____

_____

Read James 2:23.

Person: _____

Summary: _____

_____

Read Proverbs 9:9.

Person: _____

Summary: _____

_____

Who encouraged you most? Circle that person's name above and then ask the Lord for strength in walking in *righteousness*.

A.C.T.S. Prayer Time

"And the Scripture was fulfilled which saith, Abraham believed God, and it was imputed unto him for righteousness: and he was called the Friend of God."
James 2:23 King James Version

A (Adoration)
"Dear Lord, You are..._____"

C (Confession)
"I am sorry for..._____"

T (Thanksgiving)
"Thank You for..._____"

S (Supplication)
"Please help me..._____"

DAY FOUR

ON MY KNEES:

Hello! It is so great that you are back and ready to study God's Word. Pray first and then begin your study.

PRAY

"Oh, yes, Lord…You are God and there is no other like YOU! Help me see Your hand in my life. I want my life to bring glory to Your name. In Jesus' name, I pray." (Isaiah 46:9-11)

WRITE

Copy 1 John 3:22-24 on the next lines in your Sword Study pages.

READ

Once again, with a cheerful attitude, read 1 John 3 aloud to yourself.

INVESTIGATIVE STUDY
UNDER THE RUG: WORD STUDY -
"RIGHTEOSNESS"

Apply!

There is a perfect example of a **righteous** man. His name is Jesus! We have reserved today for looking at Jesus' example in Scripture. Jesus became flesh ("manifested," which means appeared) to be the payment for our sins, but He also came to show us how to live in a way that was pleasing to His Father. He was the perfect example of **righteousness** and being **righteous**!

Follow the same pattern you did yesterday. Look up the passages and fill in the blanks. There is one change, this time instead of writing the person's name, note the way Jesus shows you how to act **righteously**. Charge!

Matthew 12:49-50

Characteristic: _____

Summary: _____

_____

Matthew 20:26-28

Characteristic: _____

Summary: _____

_____

Ephesians 4:32

Characteristic: _____

Summary: _____

_____

Philippians 2:14-16

Characteristic: _____

Summary: _____

_____

Colossians 3:12-14

Characteristic: _____

Summary: _____

_____

Jesus is our Savior, Master and Brother. As you looked at His example of **righteousness**, what do you find the most difficult for you to do? Go to Him in prayer. Share with Jesus how you desire to be more like Him.

A.C.T.S. Prayer Time

"Give instruction to a wise man and he will be still wiser, teach a righteous man and he will increase his learning." Proverbs 9:9 New American Standard Version

A (Adoration)
"Dear Lord, You are..._____"

C (Confession)
"I am sorry for..._____"

T (Thanksgiving)
"Thank You for..._____"

S (Supplication)
"Please help me..._____"

DAY FIVE

ON MY KNEES:

We are here! We have arrived at the end of another week and a Day 10 Diagram. Before we begin coloring and filling in the Diagram, ask the Lord to make the lessons of 1 John 3 clear to you.

PRAY

"Father, I know that You will work in me for the best. Help me to do what is right. I want to be like Jesus. Amen."

WRITE

Look over your handwritten copy of 1 John 3. Have you marked all the references to God?

READ

Take a break from reading 1 John today and go right to working on your Day 10 Diagram.

1-2-3 CHAPTER 3 – SUMMARIZE!

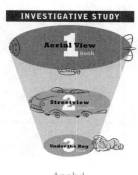

Apply!

We have arrived at another "Day 10 Diagram" summary! Take a quick look back at the first two Diagrams. Think about the summaries of the first two chapters of 1 John. Now, complete your Diagram for 1 John 3.

☐ To begin, look at the top of the Day 10 Diagram. Fill in the chapter number. Look at Week 1, Day 5 for the original title you created for 1 John 3. Review what you wrote and refine your title with the new insights that you have learned over the last 10 days.

☐ Next, which verse from the chapter do you think was the "key verse?"

☐ On the right of the page, transfer your key Greek words from this chapter. Write the English words on the top line after the words "Greek Words." Transfer the Greek spellings and write a short definition of their meanings.

☐ On the bottom of the Diagram page, transfer the most important things that you learned about God through marking the references about Him on your "Write!" pages.

In Chapter 3 of his letter, John continues to highlight the contrast between living in God's light and living in darkness. Our fellow believers in the Day 10 Diagram have chosen to "walk in the light as God is in the light." On the line above the lighthouse, label their side of the chasm, "Light." Fill in the blanks on the lighthouse with your favorite attributes of God that were mentioned in 1 John 3. "Darkness" is an apt title for the opposite side of the chasm, where those opposed to God abide. Put the word on the line within the clouds.

In 1 John 3, John has taught the Christian recipients (and us!) about the differences between the children of God and the children of the devil. On the first blank under the lighthouse, write, "Children of God" and list three things John says about these beloved, adopted children of God's family. The three descriptions of the "Children of the devil" (write that title on the top blank on the opposite side of the page) are very different- list three things John shared about this other group in Chapter 3. Some of the descriptions are in verses 10, 12 and 15.

The magnificent cross is the only bridge across the eternally deep chasm, and highlights the heart of God- indeed, as John proclaims, "God is _____." (Fill in the missing word on your diagram.) Color the heart on the cross red and write a passage reference that is your favorite description of God's love for you.

On which side have you chosen to abide?

A.C.T.S. Prayer Time

"See what kind of love the Father has given to us, that we should be called children of God; and so we are. The reason why the world does not know us is that it did not know him." 1 John 3:1 English Standard Version

A (Adoration)

" _____ "

C (Confession)

" _____ "

T (Thanksgiving)

" _____ "

S (Supplication)

" _____ "

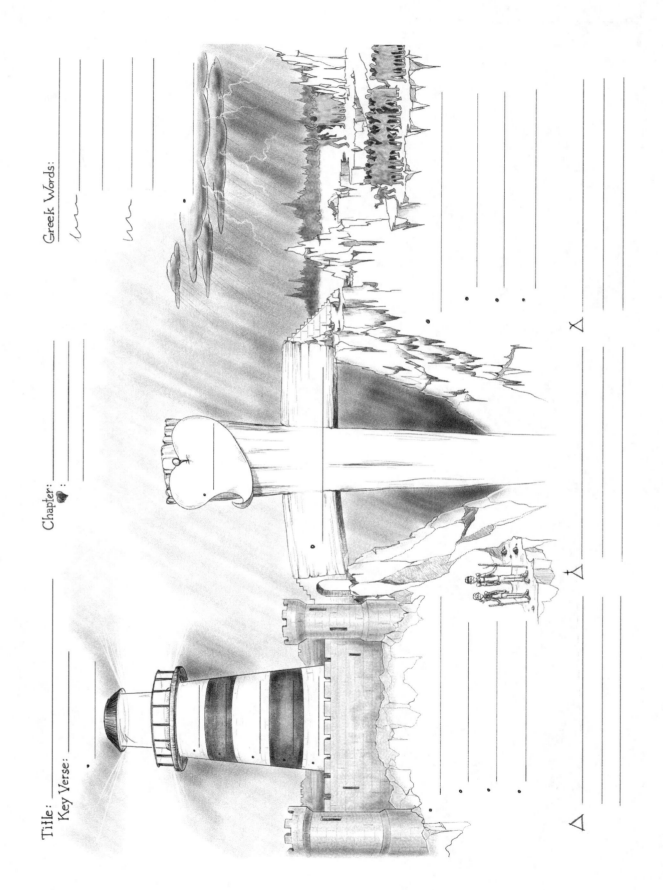

Title: _____

Key Verse: _____

Chapter: _____
     : _____

Greek Words: _____

145

Corrie ten Boom: Light in a Dark Era

Corrie ten Boom, a watchmaker, was imprisoned by the Nazis February 28, 1944 for assisting Jews in her native Holland. She and other family members endured horrible conditions and terrible treatment. After her release, Corrie never stopped proclaiming the gospel of Christ and the message of forgiveness. In this series of fictional letters (based on true events) shared from the concentration camp, she tells part of her story.

March 3, 1944

My dear friends,

I have no idea if you will receive these writings or not. I will keep them short so as to avoid the guards' prying eyes. But in a day when lies have overtaken our precious Holland, I want to speak the truth. And I want to continue to share the deep love of my Father in heaven.

These may well be the only love letters I will ever write.

My family has a long history of service to our God and His people. My great-grandfather Willem, a watchmaker like me, owned the clock shop he passed down to my father, Casper ten Boom. Willem loved God's holy people and held meetings to "pray for the peace of Jerusalem." My father held the same kind of meetings and taught us as children to love the Savior and pray for the Jewish people. What that would come to mean, only time would tell.

I can write no more now. I send this with deep love and affection.

Your sister,

Corrie

April 14, 1944

Beloved of the Lord,

And so you are. He loves you with an everlasting love, and His love underlies all earthly loves.

How did we come here? I will tell you a little more. Our family never stopped caring for the Jews. We studied their language. We celebrated their feasts. They knew us always as their friends.

Times grew hard, and the Nazis worked to destroy God's people. It seemed only natural for the sons and daughters of Israel to turn to us.

First, I helped find places for them to stay in the countryside. And before long, we ten Booms were opening our home to Jews who needed refuge. I had a false wall built in my bedroom so I could hide people there. And soon, I was helping others hide these suffering servants as well.

What we did broke the Nazis' law. But God's law is higher. My family and I could not turn away from His people, and we trust that, even here in prison, He will never turn His back on us.

In faith,

Corrie

June 6, 1944

Dear Ones,

Since my last letter, the Nazis have sent us to another prison where they have brought many more of my fellow Hollanders. I do not know whether or not they, like my family, were aiding Jews.

We have little time to talk without someone listening. And when we do, my sister Betsie (whom I now see at times) and I try to share the knowledge of God. Knowing Him is the only way to true love and abundant life—even in prison. From our earliest days, our parents passed down this truth.

Papa, like Jesus, often taught through story. As a young girl, I feared the death of one or more family members. Many of them suffered from poor health.

But my Papa asked me, "When we take the train to Amsterdam, when do I give you the ticket?"

"Just before we get on the train."

"And so God will give you the courage to carry the pain when the time comes for someone to die. Until then you should not carry it."

Papa's wisdom helps Betsie and me as we live for the Lord here behind the prison walls. And it helps us shoulder the pain of his passing. We have learned he died only ten days after imprisonment.

I must go before a guard finds me writing. I will share more at another time.

Trusting Him,
Corrie

July 12, 1944
Dear Friends,

And how did we come here, you ask? Did the guards find Jews hidden in our household? Did one of our number break down and reveal our many actions on behalf of God's chosen people?

No. What happened proved much more painful. A man came into the shop and said he and his wife had been hiding Jews. The police had taken her to jail, and he needed money to bribe an officer. I had little but gave him what I had.

A few short hours later, the Nazis came to our home to arrest us. This man was no partner in our work. He had betrayed us. In all, thirty-five people were arrested that day. My one consolation: the six Jews tucked into the hiding place in my bedroom remained free.

God cared for them. And He cares for us here in this prison.

I will tell more of the story as He grants me the time and freedom.

With gratitude,
Corrie

Learn more about God's powerful provision for Corrie and her fellow prisoners next week!

DAY ONE

ON MY KNEES:

We are starting a new chapter of 1 John today! You are growing as a child of God by studying His Word each day. Investigating the Scriptures takes hard work, so keep up the great effort! Start your week with prayer.

PRAY

"You are God, the One who sits above the earth. You stretched out the heavens like a curtain. There is no one equal to You. You do not ever get tired. Please strengthen me, Lord. Amen."

WRITE

Turn to a new page in the "Write!" portion of your Sword Study and write 1 John 4:1.

READ

Turn from your well-read pages of Chapter 3 to Chapter 4 and read all 21 verses before beginning your study. Do you have your colored pencils ready? We want you to mark the word "love" as you read by circling it with your red pencil.

INVESTIGATIVE STUDY
STREETVIEW: CHAPTER 4

Apply!

Are you ready, young investigator, for a new chapter with new questions to ask? Let's get started!

Us and Them – How to Know
Chapter 4, verses 1-8

According to 1 John 4:1, should we trust everyone who says they have wisdom from God? _____

Why? _____

According to verse 2, what does a person with the Spirit of God confess?

_____

How can we know if someone has the spirit of the antichrist, according to verse 3?

_____

According to verse 4, whose spirit is greater? _____

What three things do we learn about the antichrists in verse 5?

_____

In verse 6, what two spirits are described?

The Spirit of_____and spirit of_____.

In verse 7, we are given a command. What is it?

_____

Using verse 8, finish this sentence: God is... _____

    You are doing so well! Tomorrow, we have a special activity. Plan to invite a friend, sibling, grandparent or parent to join you in doing your Sword Study.

A.C.T.S. Prayer Time

"I will extol You, my God, O King; and I will bless Your name forever and ever. Every day I will bless You, and I will praise Your name forever and ever. Great is the Lord, and greatly to be praised; and His greatness is unsearchable."
Psalm 145:1-3 New King James Version

A (Adoration)

"Dear Lord, You are..._____"

C (Confession)

"I am sorry for..._____"

T (Thanksgiving)

"Thank You for..._____"

S (Supplication)

"Please help me..._____"

D A Y   T W O
ON MY KNEES:

Greetings, explorers! (You have asked a friend or family member to join you, right? If not, go get someone now!) Today, it is good to have the two of you together to dig in God's Word. Begin by praying.

PRAY

"Father, You are so loving and kind to give us friends with whom we can enjoy studying the Bible. Thank you for giving us friends to encourage us. We can see how John had great joy in the fellowship of God's people. Teach us from 1 John today. In Jesus' name we pray, amen."

WRITE

Turn to your "Write!" section and show your friend your copy of 1 John. Now, ask them to read 1 John 4:2-3 out loud to you as you copy. If there are any special words, explain the symbol to them as you mark the word.

READ

Before beginning your INVESTIGATIVE STUDY, read Chapter 4 of 1 John. Take turns reading four verses each.

INVESTIGATIVE STUDY
STREETVIEW: CHAPTER 4

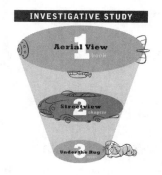

Us and Them – How to Know, continued.
Chapter 4, verses 1-8

Yesterday, we questioned the first eight verses of 1 John 4. Today, we will look at some of the same verses in a different way. We have taken a few words from each verse and found them somewhere else in the Bible.

You read the verse from 1 John 4. Your friend will read the passage listed next to it. Together answer the questions for each pair of verses. Have a good time fellowshipping in God's Word.

1 John 4, Verse 1: "Many false prophets"...see 2 Peter 2:1.

What things do false prophets do? _____

_____

1 John 4, Verse 3: "The spirit that does not confess"...see 2 John 7

What do the deceivers say about Jesus? _____

_____

1 John 4, Verse 4: "Greater is He"... see Romans 8:38-39

Is there anything powerful enough to separate us from God's love?

_____

Name the things that cannot separate us from the love of God: _____

_____

_____

1 John 4, Verse 6: "Who listens to God"...see John 10:3-4

Why do the sheep follow the shepherd? _____

_____

Who is like a shepherd?_____ Who are like sheep?_____

APPLY!

Ready to be an artist? Great! Gather two pencils, two pieces of plain paper, and one sibling or friend. Take turns drawing one another. After you have both done your portraits, turn your pages over and write five reasons the other person is special to you. Finally, present your papers to one another as a gift!

Praise the Lord together using the passage listed in your A.C.T.S. prayer section. Don't forget to tell the Lord and your friend how much you appreciate him or her!

A.C.T.S. Prayer Time

"For my brothers and companions' sake I will say, "Peace be within you!"
For the sake of the house of the Lord our God, I will seek your good."
Psalm 122:8-9 English Standard Version

A (Adoration)
"Dear Lord, You are..._____"

C (Confession)
"I am sorry for..._____"

T (Thanksgiving)
"Thank You for..._____"

S (Supplication)
"Please help me..._____"

DAY THREE
ON MY KNEES:

Are you feeling good? Or are you feeling sad? You probably had a great time having a friend study with you yesterday. The Lord loves fellowshipping with you, too. You can always share your true feelings with the Lord. He is able to handle how we feel, whether good or bad. Go speak with Him through prayer.

PRAY

"Father, You alone hear my thoughts, cries and feelings with patience and per-fect love. I want to deepen my relationship with You because You are the best of friends. Place Your words on my heart. In Jesus' name I pray, amen."

WRITE

1 John 4:6-7 on the next lines of your "Write" section.

READ

Once again, please read Chapter 4 of 1 John.

INVESTIGATIVE STUDY
STREETVIEW: CHAPTER 4

"What is God's Love?"
Chapter 4, verses 9 - 21

Today, we are back to finish our questioning of 1 John 4 verses. So, carry on!

1 John 4, Verses 9-11:

What has God done because of His love, according to verse 9?

According to verse 10, why was Jesus sent into the world?

_____

Since God loved us, what should we do, according to verse 11?

_____

Verses 12-16:

According to verse 12, has God ever been seen?

_____

Why did the Father send the Son, according to verse 14?

_____

According to verse 15, what happens if we confess that Jesus is God's Son?

_____

Verses 17-21:

What four things do we learn about fear in verse 18?

_____   _____

_____   _____

Why do we love God, according to verse 19?

_____

According to verse 21, what are we commanded to do if we love God?

_____

A.C.T.S. PRAYER TIME

"And I said: "I pray, Lord God of heaven, O great and awesome God, You who keep Your covenant and mercy with those who love You and observe Your commandments,"
Nehemiah 1:5 New King James Version

A (Adoration)
"Dear Lord, You are..._____"

C (Confession)
"I am sorry for..._____"

T (Thanksgiving)
"Thank You for..._____"

S (Supplication)
"Please help me..._____"

DAY FOUR

ON MY KNEES:

Before you start, can you go get a second Bible? Okay, let's jump right in and start our time with Jesus by praying.

PRAY

"Lord...You always succeed. I praise You for the great things Your Word does for me. Thank You for giving me Your Word so I can be strengthened by it."

WRITE

Neatly write 1 John 4:8.

READ

Once again, read 1 John 4.

INVESTIGATIVE STUDY STREETVIEW: CHAPTER 4

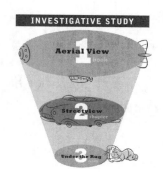

Apply!

"What is God's Love?"
Chapter 4, verses 9 - 21

Have you guessed what we are going to do today? Now, we are going to look at verses 9 through 21 again. We will match them with other verses with the same phrases.

Open your Bible to the 1 John verse and use the second Bible to find the matching passage. After you read both passages, then answer the questions.

1 John 4, Verse 10: "He loves us"...see Romans 5:8

When we were still sinners, what did God do for us?_____

1 John 4, Verse 12: "No one has seen God"....see 1 Timothy 6:16

Where does God dwell?_____

1 John 4, Verse 14: "The Father has sent the Son"…see John 3:17

Why did God send Jesus into the world?_____

1 John 4, Verse 15: "Whoever confesses"…see Romans 10:9

What two things must a person do to be saved? Fill-in the blanks.

They must confess:_____ and believe:_____.

1 John 4, Verse 21: "This commandment we have"…see Matthew 22:37-39

What is the first commandment?_____

_____

What is the second commandment?_____

A.C.T.S. Prayer Time

"Jesus said unto him, Thou shalt love the Lord thy God with all thy heart, and with all thy soul, and with all thy mind. This is the first and great commandment."
Matthew 22:37-3 King James Version

A (Adoration)
"Dear Lord, You are..._____ "

C (Confession)
"I am sorry for..._____ "

T (Thanksgiving)
"Thank You for..._____ "

S (Supplication)
"Please help me..._____ "

DAY FIVE
ON MY KNEES:

God loves to see you choose to spend time with Him. Begin with prayer and then dive right into your Bible.

PRAY

"Lord, You give me light and truth in Your Word; let them lead me to live in a holy way. When I am down or worried, remind me of what I have in You. You are my salvation and my God. Give me joy as we spend time together today. In Your powerful name, I pray."

WRITE

Grab your pencil and begin to write 1 John 4:9-10 in the "Write!" section of your Sword Study.

READ

Ask a parent if you can call one of your grandparents or another relative. Read 1 John 4 to them as your reading assignment for the day.

INVESTIGATIVE STUDY
STREETVIEW: CHAPTER 4

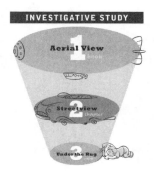

Apply!

We want to look at all the things that John is teaching us about God and His Son, Jesus. We are going to do this by marking the first ten verses of 1 John Chapter 4. Using the symbols below, mark all the words for God, Jesus and the Holy Spirit that you find in 1 John 4:1-10. Do this on YOUR handwritten copy in the back of your Sword Study.

GOD
the Father

GOD
the Son

GOD
the Holy Spirit

Today is a catch-up day! Have you been marking the words for God on all of your chapters? Go back over your copy on the "Write" pages and make sure to mark every word that represents God, Jesus or the Holy Spirit. Don't forget to mark the pronouns, too. Those are words like "He" and "Him."

Every Bible verse can teach us so much!

A.C.T.S. Prayer Time

Finish your Bible study time telling the Lord what you have learned about Him.

A (Adoration)
"Dear Lord, You are..._____"

C (Confession)
"I am sorry for..._____"

T (Thanksgiving)
"Thank You for..._____"

S (Supplication)
"Please help me..._____"

Corrie ten Boom: Light in a Dark Era (continued)

September 18, 1944

Precious Partners,

Betsie and I remain so grateful for your prayers. We have been transferred to another prison, Ravensbruck, and see each other much more often now.

In this place, prisoners care for one another in small but large ways, sharing a thin blanket or a crust of bread.

Betsie remains herself. She serves and loves each one with God's deep love. She has that kind, tender affection Scripture encourages us to have.

I, on the other hand, am far more selfish. But I remain so grateful for our loving Lord. He has allowed us to keep a small Bible in our tiny collection of belongings.

When we entered the prison, I hid it on my back under my clothing. But I feared the guards would take it away. I said, "O Lord, send Your angels, that they surround me."

And then I thought, Yes, but angels are spirits and you can look through a spirit. So I told Him, "O God, let Your angels this time not be transparent."

And He did! The guards searched the woman in front of me. They searched my sister, right behind me. But the angels covered me, and the guards did not see me. I entered the prison with my Bible.

Praising Him,

Corrie

November 8, 1944

Dear Fellow Servants of the King,

My sister and I continue to serve from behind the prison walls. Here, we have the privilege of holding small worship services in praise of our Lord. We thank Him for the fleas because they keep the guards from entering our cell block. Our loving Father brings light into darkness—even through the fleas.

At one point, the guards gave me a vision test to see if I could perform another type of labor. I knew Betsie had no such strength. I made sure I missed most of the questions. God watched out for me, and I am now assigned to knitting duty right beside my beloved sister.

God continues to perform miracles on our behalf. Food is scarce and many, including my sweet Betsie, have grown very thin. I am sharing my old bottle of vitamins, hoping to keep up everyone's strength despite the poor rations. Every day, I think the supply will end, and every day, more vitamins remain.

He is Lord,

Corrie

December 3, 1944

Dear Saints,

Betsie grows frailer by the day. However, she still manages to serve others and encourage them in the Lord. She also takes time to share with me her vision for the future: "Sister, we will have a house again—a house that will help those damaged by these camps. We will serve both the prisoners and the guards, anyone whose life has suffered the trauma of this time in history."

Her ability to envision a life outside the camp amazes me. I have difficulty thinking beyond our daily bread. But Betsie uses her heart to see God's plan for good and not for evil, to give us a future and a hope.

Truly, my sister loves with the sacrificial love of Christ. Her willingness to pray for even our captors—who treat us with indifference at best and cruelty at worst—shows the depth of her love.

I often pray, "Lord, make me more like You." Today, could You make me a little more like Betsie, too?

In hopeful expectation,

Corrie

December 17, 1944

Our Family,

Today's news weighs heavy on my heart.

Betsie now has a life outside the camp. She stands strong and whole with our Lord in heaven.

Yesterday, when she could no longer rise for roll call, a friend and I carried her out. Later, we returned her to bed. Although those in charge had already denied permission, one guard cared enough to admit her to the hospital.

I visited at noon and found her resting. That evening, the guards would not allow me to visit. I peered through the hospital window and realized she lay dead. My sweet, caring sister no longer had to bear the pain of the camp or the concerns of others. Her face showed her peace.

And with this, I could let her go.

Trusting Him,

Corrie

Through a clerical error, Corrie ten Boom was released from Ravensbruck three days after her sister found her final freedom. She made her way back to Holland, received care in a hospital, and returned to their former home in Haarlem. Corrie began to speak out about the horrors of the concentration camps and how God had held her close.

She used every meeting as a way to share Betsie's vision for a home to help people heal from wartime trauma. She received financial gifts along with the donation of a home almost identical to the one her sister had envisioned. Its first residents were those who had been hidden away as well as those who had been imprisoned.

Corrie spent the rest of her life telling Betsie's story. Eventually, she moved to the United States. She wrote seven books, including The Hiding Place, which also became a movie. Until her death in 1983, Corrie ten Boom preached the messages of sacrificial love and forgiveness lived out by her sister Betsie. She became a true light in a dark era.

DAY ONE

ON MY KNEES:

Hi! We are so glad you are back to study God's Word. Go to Jesus in prayer and then you can start a new week of investigating.

PRAY

"God, use Your Holy Spirit to work in me so I understand the words of 1 John today. I am kind of tired from a fun weekend. Help me pay attention to Your words. In Jesus' name, I pray, amen."

WRITE

Please write 1 John 4:11-13 in your copy of 1 John.

READ

Open up your Bible to 1 John and read Chapter 4.

INVESTIGATIVE STUDY
UNDER THE RUG: WORD STUDY - "LOVE"

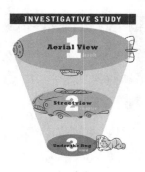

Apply!

Beloved. This is like John saying, "Dear Loved Ones" in his letter. He says this three times in Chapter 4. Can you see him saying it to himself as he writes it on the letter's paper? "Beloved. Love one another. God is love. He loved us."

There is no doubt that **love** is a Key Word to this chapter. Actually, it is a Key Word for the whole book of 1 John. We have had a hard time waiting until Chapter 4 to share the word study of **love** with you! Now, it is time.

Highlight the word **love** in your Bible from 1 John Chapter 1 all the way to the end of Chapter 5. Use a red colored pencil.

Wow! We know that may have taken you a long time. How many times did John write the word **love** in 1 John? _____

APPLY!

List the people in your life that you love. After you have finished writing down the names, pray for the first four people during your prayer time. Pray for the next four tomorrow, the next four day after tomorrow, and so on until you have prayed for your list.

_____   _____   _____   _____

_____   _____   _____   _____

_____   _____   _____   _____

_____   _____   _____   _____

_____   _____   _____   _____

A.C.T.S. PRAYER TIME

"By this all men will know that you are My disciples, if you have love for one another."
John 13:35 New American Standard Version

A (Adoration)
"Dear Lord, You are..._____"

C (Confession)
"I am sorry for..._____"

T (Thanksgiving)
"Thank You for..._____"

S (Supplication)
"Please help me..._____"

D A Y   T W O

ON MY KNEES:

Love. I love chocolate. I love this game. I love dogs. God is love. One of these things just isn't like the others! We are going to learn about the word "love" this week. Let's start with prayer.

PRAY

"God, You are able to do far more than what I ask or can even think to ask, teach me what You meant when You said You were love, and I am to love others. I want to learn to love like You. Amen."

WRITE

As you write 1 John 4:14-16, don't forget to mark all the references to God.

READ

Grab your mom or dad and read Chapter 4 aloud with each other, taking turns every three verses or so.

INVESTIGATIVE STUDY
UNDER THE RUG: WORD STUDY - "LOVE"

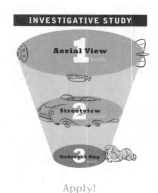

Apply!

Before we move to the word study of **love**, finish marking the word **love** in Chapter 4 of your Bible.

In English we have only one word to describe what **love** could mean. Usually context helps us here. You don't **love** your mom the same way you **love** pizza! The Greek uses four different words for the word **love**: storgay, eros, phileo, and agape. We will examine them in this order.

Storgay

This word for **love** does not appear in the New Testament, but it is found inside a compound word (with phileo) in Romans 12:10. we also find a negative word from it in Romans 1:31 and 2 Timothy 3:3.

PART A: As we look up the word *kindly affectionate/devoted/love* in the Strong's Concordance, we find that the Strong's number assigned to it in Romans 12:10 is 5387. Below is how we write the word in the English language, the pronunciation, and then the basic definition from the Strong's dictionary.

5387. Love. philostorgos. *fil-os'-tor-gos*; from 5384 and storge: cherishing one's family or fellow Christian

PART B: We will now look up the number 5387 in another Greek dictionary to discover a more detailed explanation of the word *kindly affectionate/devoted/love* in Greek:

1) the mutual love of parents and children and wives and husbands
2) loving affection, prone to love, loving tenderly
    a) chiefly of the reciprocal tenderness of parents and children

Eros

PART A: Eros also does not appear in the New Testament. Therefore, we won't find a Strong's number attached to it. But the way we write the word in English and basic definition can be found below. We generally think of this kind of love as the romantic love between a husband and a wife.

1) **Love.** eros. *air-ohs, noun*; love, desire

Phileo

PART A: As we look up this word for *love* in the Strong's Concordance, we find that the Strong's number assigned to it in John 21:17 is 5368. Below is the English word, the pronunciation, and then the basic definition from the Strong's dictionary.

5368. Love. phileo. *fil-eh'-o*; from 5384: to be a friend

PART B: We will now look up the number 5368 in another Greek lexicon to discover a more detailed explanation of the Greek word **phileo**:

> 1) to love
>> a) to approve of
>> b) to like
>> c) to treat affectionately or kindly, to welcome, befriend
> 2) to show signs of love

Agape

PART A: As we look up the word **charity/love[ing]** in the Strong's Concordance, we find that the Strong's number assigned to it in 1 John 4:8 is 26. Below is the way in which we write the word in the English language, the pronunciation, and then the basic definition from the Strong's dictionary.

> **26. Love.** agape. ag-ah'-pay; from 25: love, i.e. affection or benevolence, charity, dear, love.

PART B: We will now look up the number 26 in another Greek lexicon to discover a more detailed explanation of the word **charity/love[ing]** in Greek:

> 1) affection, good will, love.
> 2) benevolent. This love is shown by the loved recieving what they **need** versus what they may **want**.
> 3) unconditional, self-sacrificing

PART C: The Strong's definition says that the main difference between the last two Greek words for **love** is that **agapao** (verb form of **agape**) is a matter of the head, and **phileo** is a matter of the heart. **Agape love** always involves God! He is the only One who can **love** perfectly, His Holy Spirit helps us to **love** like he loves people. Don't forget to pray for a few more of the people you **love** from your "Apply!" list you wrote yesterday.

A.C.T.S. Prayer Time

"So now faith, hope, and love abide, these three; but the greatest of these is love."
1 Corinthians 13:13 ESV

A (Adoration)
"Dear Lord, You are..._____"

C (Confession)
"I am sorry for..._____"

T (Thanksgiving)
"Thank You for..._____"

S (Supplication)
"Please help me..._____"

DAY THREE

ON MY KNEES:

How are you doing today, young explorer? Remember, there is nothing too difficult for the Lord. We need to lean on His strength. Let's go before Him in prayer.

PRAY

"According to Genesis 18:14, there is nothing too difficult for You, Lord! In Your name, I pray for strength to live today in Your way. Through Your Spirit, help me act in ways that reflect Your light. In Your Almighty name, I pray. Amen."

WRITE

Prayerfully write 1 John 4:17-19. Think about the words as you write.

READ

Before you begin your word study, please read Chapter 4 of 1 John.

INVESTIGATIVE STUDY
UNDER THE RUG: CROSS REFERENCES - "LOVE"

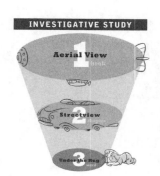

Apply!

Every time we see the word **love** in 1 John, it is the Greek word **agape**! John says that we are known by our **love**. He says God's children **love** others. Here are some great verses that tell us more about **love**. Look them up and fill in your answers to the questions.

Read Matthew 5:43-44.

Who man says we should **love**: _____

Who God says we should **love**: _____

Read Matthew 22:37-38.

God says **love**: _____

Fill in the blanks: This is the_____and_____ commandment.

Read John 3:16.

Fill in the blanks: God so **loved** the world that He:_____ Son.

Read 2 Corinthians 5:14-15*.

What does the **love** of Christ do to us? _____

For whom are we supposed to live? (1 line) _____

Read Ephesians 5:1-4*.

How do children of God walk? _____

Who is their example? _____

How should they talk? _____

_____

Have you ever heard the saying, "you need to walk your talk?" God wants us to walk and talk like Jesus did when He was on earth. We need to act like God's children so others see Jesus' light.

APPLY!

Who do you know that acts a lot like Jesus?

Write his or her name here: _____

Make a list of the things that this person does that reminds you of how Jesus would act and write them on the lines below.

_____

_____

_____

Walking like Jesus can be hard, so close your Bible study by praying for God's help to be like Jesus.

A.C.T.S. PRAYER TIME

"And walk in love, as Christ loved us and gave himself up for us, a fragrant offering and sacrifice to God." Ephesians 5:2 English Standard Version

A (Adoration)
"Dear Lord, You are..._____"

C (Confession)
"I am sorry for..._____"

T (Thanksgiving)
"Thank You for..._____"

S (Supplication)
"Please help me..._____"

D A Y   F O U R

ON MY KNEES:

Shhh, quietly go to the Lord in prayer before continuing your study of the word *love*.

PRAY

"How AWESOME Lord to know that You can do ALL things and that NO purpose of Yours can be stopped. Praise You, Lord! For no man, whether strong or weak, wealthy or poor, wise or foolish can block Your purposes!"

WRITE

Write 1 John 4:20-21 to finish your copy of 1 John, Chapter 4.

READ

Open your Bible to 1 John 4 and read all 21 verses.

INVESTIGATIVE STUDY
UNDER THE RUG: CROSS REFERENCES - "LOVE"

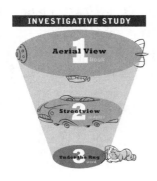

Apply!

God's **agape love** tells us to **love** even when we don't feel like it. So even when we are mad or hurt, God still says, "**Love** one another." God's **love** is perfect. He always **loves** perfectly. He **loves** us regardless of how we act. Today, we will look at more **love** cross references.

Read Deuteronomy 6:5-7.
What were the important words the fathers were to teach their children? _____

_____

Read John 13:35.
How do people know that we are Jesus' followers? _____

Love is so important that God used a whole chapter of the Bible to give us His definition. He wants us to know exactly what He calls love. If we are going to show others Jesus' love, we need to know how love acts. This chapter tells us how to love.

Do the activities below. (If you are using the King James Version, look for the word charity)

Read 1 Corinthians 13.

☐ Circle or put a heart around the word love (charity) using a red colored pencil.

☐ Underline the all the things that love (charity) does. Hint: Look at the words right after Love is...

☐ Beloved, student of the Bible, be sure to love your mom, dad, siblings and family using what you have learned in this chapter. Sometimes it is hard. Ask Jesus to help you love like He does when you pray today.

A.C.T.S. Prayer Time

"But as it is written: 'Eye has not seen, nor ear heard, nor have entered into the heart of man the things which God has prepared for those who love Him.'"
1 Corinthians 2:9 New King James Version

A (Adoration)
"Dear Lord, You are..._____"

C (Confession)
"I am sorry for..._____"

T (Thanksgiving)
"Thank You for..._____"

S (Supplication)
"Please help me..._____"

D A Y   F I V E
O N   M Y   K N E E S :

What is on your schedule for the day? As you pray before your Bible study, ask the Lord to show you ways to love others.

PRAY

"Lord, You love me. I know this is true because I believe You sent Your Son, Jesus, to die for my sins. I saw yesterday how you want me to love others. Help me to show love to my family like You do. In Your loving Name, I pray, amen."

WRITE

Take a few minutes to review Chapter 4. Are there any references to God? Be sure to mark them with the symbols.

READ

It is Day 10 Diagram Day! Read 1 John 4, one more time.

1 - 2 - 3   S U M M A R I Z E :   CHAPTER 4

Apply!

You have completed the study of another chapter of 1 John. Once again, we will summarize the main theme, Greek words and attributes that the Lord has taught us by completing a Day 10 Diagram. Before you begin to work through Chapter 4, briefly look at your first three Diagrams.

☐ To begin, look at the top of the Day 10 Diagram. Fill in the chapter number. Look at Week 1, Day 5 for the original title you created for 1 John 4. Review what you wrote and refine your title with the new insights that you have learned over the last 10 days.

☐ Next, which verse from the chapter do you think was the "key verse?"

☐ On the right of the page, transfer the Greek word **agape** and its definition on the first two lines. Then, place the other three Greek words for love and their definitions on the next three lines.

☐ On the bottom of the Diagram page, transfer the most important things that you learned about God through marking the references about Him on your "Write!" pages.

We learned in 1 John 4 that God is **love**. As we abide in Christ, His **love** grows strong in and through us just like this mighty 1 Corinthians 13 tree. Our young sister in Christ is studying that chapter of the Bible as she rests in the refreshing shelter of God's **agape love**. On the ripe fruit in the branches of the tree, write the six qualities describing what she reads **love** IS according to 1 Corinthians. Write the nine qualities that 1 Corinthians says **love** IS NOT beside the rotten, fallen apples scattered on the ground.

Those bad apples more aptly characterize the "Darkness" of the world- add that label on the storm clouds hovering over the horizon. In Chapter 4 of his letter, what four descriptions did John give for those who don't belong to God? Write them on the lines below the dark clouds. (Hint: Verses 1, 3 and 20)

The darkness can't diminish the beauty and strength of God's incredible **love**, however. Along the sturdy trunk and branches of the tree, trace the outline of the cross, because the cross of Christ is God's greatest demonstration of His sacrificial **love**. In the heart on the trunk, "carve" John's message in 1 John 4:10 about Who **loved** whom first. How wonderful that we also can rest in God's eternal **love**, day by day, and then share His kind of **love** with all those around us!

A.C.T.S. Prayer Time

"I will bless the LORD who has counseled me; indeed, my mind instructs me in the night. I have set the LORD continually before me; because He is at my right hand, I will not be shaken. Therefore my heart is glad and my glory rejoices; my flesh also will dwell securely." Psalm 16:7-9 New American Standard Bible

A (Adoration)

"Dear Lord, You are..._____ "

C (Confession)

"I am sorry for..._____ "

T (Thanksgiving)

"Thank You for..._____ "

S (Supplication)

"Please help me..._____ "

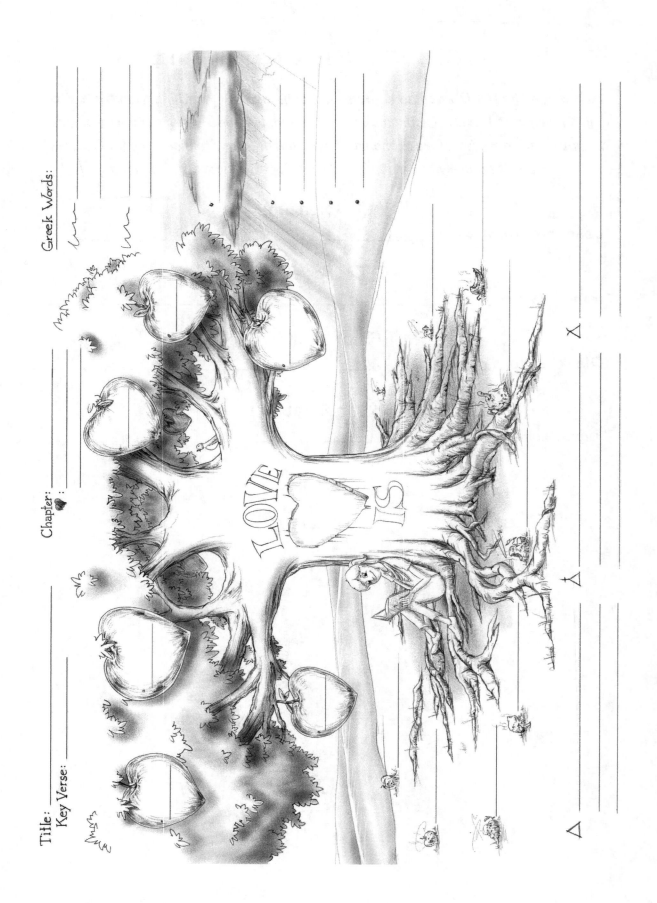

Title:

Chapter:

Key Verse:

Greek Words:

Martin Luther: Table Talk

Who sits at your dinner table? Through the years, Reformer Martin Luther and his wife Katharina hosted many students, famous reformers, and others at their home in Germany. The conversations often became so spirited that many of the guests took notes. Some of these conversations were later compiled in Table Talk, still one of Luther's most popular books.

This week and next, our Shelby Kennedy Foundation representatives Anne (13) and Grace (9) visit the Luther home to ask the special questions inquiring Sword Study minds want to know.

Anne: Dr. Luther, of course I know who you are, but could you give our Sword Study students some insight into how God uses you?

Luther: Most gladly, my child. First of all, I identify myself as a teacher of truth. In the same way that I host great thinkers at my table, our world plays host to any number of lies. I see it as my calling to combat those lies as I stand for the truths of God's Word.

Grace: But why would people lie, Dr. Luther? I don't understand.

Luther: Ahh, of course you would not comprehend this, dear one. Why do people lie? Because of the curse of sin and death that hangs over this world. Because the evil one comes to steal, kill and destroy. And because men love to believe they are right at the expense of anything or anyone else.

Anne: But isn't it important to get along with others, Dr. Luther? I hear you started some pretty big arguments in your day.

Luther: Someone else asked me about that, so I'll give you the answer he received: "Peace if possible. Truth at all costs." In other words, I find it more important to speak the truth than to agree with others—who may or may not have a strong commitment to the truths of God's Word.

Grace: How did you start exploring the truth, sir?

Luther: I believe I was born to explore the truth—in Eiseben, Germany on

November 10, 1843. My father sent me to Latin school and then to the University of Ehrfurst to study law.

Anne: Latin school? What's that?

Luther: Simply a school for younger pupils, my dear. This one taught the Ten Commandments, the Lord's Prayer, basic Latin grammar and the parts of the Bible used in church services at that time.

Grace: I study Latin, too, but not quite that much.

Luther: Another time, perhaps we should have a conversation in Latin. In any case, God used this early schooling to prepare me for His purposes.

Anne: You studied law. Did you become a lawyer?

Luther: As I said, God prepared me for His purposes. One evening, on my way back to school from my parents' home, a thunderstorm trapped me and a bolt of lightning struck the ground nearby. I fell to my knees, crying out, "Help me, St. Anne! I will become a monk!"

Grace: Were you scared of the storm, Dr. Luther?

Luther: Not nearly as scared of the storm as of our God. I had already been seeking Him and questioning His desires for my life. The storm and the lightning moved me toward a decision. I gave away everything I owned and entered a monastery—a place where I could live with others devoted to religious life.

Anne: And were you? Devoted to religious life, I mean?

Luther: Yes, I was. And that was part of the problem.

Grace: But how could that be a problem? Weren't you doing what God wanted you to do?

Luther: I thought I was. I was doing everything I could to try to please God: fasting, praying, and even going without good food or warm blankets. But as I spent more time studying the Scriptures, I realized my ideas of being godly looked different than God's true desires. I read, "The righteous shall live by faith" (Romans 1:17) and wondered how I could ever be righteous. But all the while, God was drawing me to Himself.

Anne: So did you move out of the monastery?

Luther: Not quite yet. My superior ordered me to become a student, so I studied and then taught theology at the University of Wittenberg. In the process, God showed me the only way to achieve righteousness was through His gift of faith. At long last, I knew I was born again. I wanted to share my learning with my others. I wanted them to know the truth!

Grace: And that kind of teaching got you in trouble, didn't it?

Luther: Yes, it did. But again—I prefer to stand for the truth. I became so passionate about the importance of faith alone as a means of grace, so burdened about the need for the common man to read the Scriptures, and so angry with the corrupt practices of the Church that on October 31, 1517, I nailed 95 Theses (statements of truth) to the door of the church at Wittenberg. Some call this the beginning of the Protestant Reformation.

Anne: Wow. When you stand for the truth, you *really* stand for the truth, don't you, Dr. Luther? I guess it's time to close our interview for now. But we'll be back again next week with some more fascinating Table Talk.

D A Y   O N E
ON MY KNEES:

You are rounding the corner and heading for home as we begin this last chapter of 1 John. You have been a diligent student of the Word. As the eyes of the Lord move to and fro looking for those who seek after Him, He sees you! Once again, begin on your knees in prayer.

PRAY

"God, You are the God who sees all things. Look into my heart and show me where I need to act more like You. Speak to me through the words of 1 John 5. Amen."

WRITE

Begin writing 1 John 5:1-2 on a new page of your "My Copy of 1 John" pages.

READ

As we start the last chapter of 1 John, take the extra time today to read all five chapters. You can do it! If you are under 9 years old, just read 1 John 5 today.

INVESTIGATIVE STUDY
STREETVIEW: CHAPTER 5

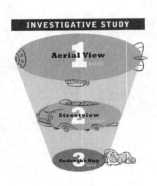

Apply!

Every time we see the word *love* in 1 John it is the Greek word *agape*! John says that we are known by our *love*. He says God's children *love* others. Here are some great verses that tell us more about *love*. Look them up and fill in your answers to the questions.

Last week we learned about God's *love*. We also saw how we can show God *love* by obeying His commandments. We learned about God's *love* by studying 1 Corinthians 13. Today, put your interviewer hat back on and let's ask "Who, What, Why, Where,

When, Which and How" questions of the verses in 1 John 5.

Who?

Who is born of God? (verse1): _____

Who overcomes the world? (verse 4): _____

Who gives eternal life? (verse11): _____

What?

What shows we love God? (verse 3): _____

What does faith do? (verse 4): _____

What is sin? (verse 17): _____

Why?

Why was 1 John written? (verse 13): _____

Where?

Where is eternal life found? (verse 11): _____

Way to press on through all those interview questions! We will finish up our interview tomorrow.

APPLY!

Create and decorate coupons for your family to show your love for them. For example, you could give a sibling a coupon to make his or her bed for a week or make an "I will do the dishes" coupon for your mom, or a coupon telling your dad that you will help him wash the car. Plan to give out your coupons at your Family Bonfire.

Next, go to the Lord in prayer. He is to be praised above all people and things.

A.C.T.S. Prayer Time

"O praise the Lord, all ye nations: praise him, all ye people. For his merciful kindness is great toward us: and the truth of the Lord endureth for ever. Praise ye the Lord."
Psalm 117:1-2 King James Version

A (Adoration)
"Dear Lord, You are..._____"

C (Confession)
"I am sorry for..._____"

T (Thanksgiving)
"Thank You for..._____"

S (Supplication)
"Please help me..._____"

DAY TWO
ON MY KNEES:

Hello! What is it like where you are doing your study? Are you at home or away from home? Praise the Lord for the nice place that you can study His Word. Let's pray.

PRAY

"God, Ruler of all nations, thank You for providing a place where I can study the Bible. I confess that I grumble about little things. I am grateful for the place I have to live, the food I have to eat and the extras that surround me. Help me focus on the things that are important to You. Thank You, Father. Amen."

WRITE

Write 1 John 5:3-5 on the next lines of your "Write" pages.

READ

Slowly read through 1 John 5 today.

INVESTIGATIVE STUDY
STREETVIEW: CHAPTER 5

Are you ready to do the rest of the interview questions for Chapter 5? Great, finish well!

INVESTIGATIVE STUDY

Aerial View
1 book

Streetview
2 chapter

Under the Rug
3

Apply!

When?

When we love God and do His commandments, what can we know? (verse 2): _____

When does God hear our prayers? (verse 14): _____

_____

Which?

Which witness is greater? (verse 9): _____

Which person has the witness/testimony in him? (verse 10): _____

_____

How?

What can we be sure of when we pray? (verse 14): _____

_____

How should we handle idols? (verse 21): _____

Wait a minute! Before we finish up, let's take a quick look at one of the words in the last verse of 1 John 5. John slips in one last command instead of saying "Goodbye" at the end of his letter. He says, "Little children, keep yourselves from idols." Then, he finishes with Amen. What is an idol?

Do you think it is a piece of wood? Or a golden calf? Maybe it is a statue? Write a short description of what you think an idol is, right here:

_____

You may be thinking that you don't have to worry about John's last command to keep yourself away from idols. Well, an idol is anything that we think of or care more about than God. God says, "Love Me most." He says, "Love the Lord, your God, with all your heart, and mind, and soul." We see the words, "You shall have NO other gods before Me," too.

Use your prayer time today to pray about anything you are placing ahead of God. If you can't think of a thing, ask Him to put a spotlight on anything that you aren't noticing.

A.C.T.S. Prayer Time

"For great is the Lord, and greatly to be praised; He is to be feared above all gods. For all the gods of the peoples are worthless idols, but the Lord made the heavens."

Psalm 96:4-5 English Standard Version

A (Adoration)
"Dear Lord, You are..._____"

C (Confession)
"I am sorry for..._____"

T (Thanksgiving)
"Thank You for..._____"

S (Supplication)
"Please help me..._____"

DAY THREE
ON MY KNEES:

How blessed is the person who walks in *God's* ways! You can be happy and things will be good on the inside even if what you are experiencing is really hard. These words are like those in Psalm 128. Let's pray and thank Him for His promises.

PRAY

"Lord, help me to trust You. Help me to look at everything as a way to make me more like Jesus. Thank You for always being with me. Amen."

WRITE

1 John 5:6-8 is your next set of verses. We suggest that you write the word "water" with a blue colored pencil.

READ

Once again, please read Chapter 5 of 1 John.

INVESTIGATIVE STUDY
STREETVIEW: CHAPTER 5

Apply!

John mentioned that Jesus had more witnesses that testify that He was God's Son. Look at 1 John 5:6-8.

What two things are listed about how Jesus came to earth from heaven?

_____

_____

We are going to zoom in on the water today. The water stands for baptism. Jesus was baptized. What is baptism? A simple definition of the word baptize is "to dip in water as a ceremony to show someone is beginning their life with

Jesus Christ." The baptism was giving an example of the water washing away the dirt (sin), coming up clean and ready to live for Jesus.

Let's look at different baptisms in the Bible to see what they are like and why people got baptized. Then, tomorrow we can look at Jesus' baptism.

Matthew 3:4-6

Who was baptizing people? _____

How did he baptize people? _____

What had the people done just before they were baptized? _____

_____

Acts 2:38

Who was baptizing people? _____

What did he tell the people to do before he would baptize them? _____

_____

When they repented, what was forgiven? _____

What gift did they receive? _____

Acts 8:12

Who was preaching and baptizing people? _____

Before they were baptized, what did they believe? _____

Tomorrow, we will look at Jesus' baptism. Before you close your Bible and put away your things, go to the Lord in prayer.

A.C.T.S. Prayer Time

"For ye are all the children of God by faith in Christ Jesus. For as many of you as have been baptized into Christ have put on Christ."
Galatians 3:26-27 King James Version

A (Adoration)
"Dear Lord, You are..._____"

C (Confession)
"I am sorry for..._____"

T (Thanksgiving)
"Thank You for..._____"

S (Supplication)
"Please help me..._____"

Digging Deeper

Look up these two passages and fill in the blanks below: Mark 3:17 and Luke 1:57-63.

John, the Baptist

Son of _____

John, the writer of 1 John and the Gospel of John

Son of _____

Are they the same person? _____

DAY FOUR

ON MY KNEES:

Surprise, the sun came up today! We know that this is probably not a surprise. Hosea 6 says just as sure as the dawn comes, so is the faithfulness of our God. Pray to your faithful God. He is waiting for you as surely as the sun rose this morning.

PRAY

"Lord, You are faithful. It is so good to know that You do not change. I am so thankful that I can depend on You. Speak to me through Your words in 1 John 5."

WRITE

Write 1 John 5:9-10.

READ

Once again, read 1 John 5.

INVESTIGATIVE STUDY STREETVIEW: CHAPTER 5

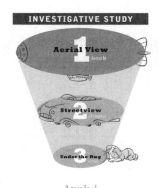

Apply!

Now that you have a better understanding of baptism, let's zoom in on the testimony of the blood. The water and the blood are connected by the baptism of Jesus.

Let's look at the book of Matthew to hear the story of Jesus' baptism. Turn to Matthew 3:11-17. Read the passage and use what you learn to answer the questions below.

Who baptized Jesus (verse 13)? _____

With what did he baptize Jesus (verse 11)? _____

With what did John say Jesus baptized (verse 11)? _____

What happened after Jesus was baptized (verse 16)? _____

_____

What did God say about Jesus (verse 17)? _____

These verses tell us of Jesus' first baptism. Jesus tells us about his second baptism. This one is not with water. Read Mark 10:38-39. Jesus mentions a cup in this passage. We are on a hunt to find out what He is talking about, so turn to Mark 14:35-36 and read the verses.

You have found the treasure at the end of the hunt! Jesus called His death on the cross for our sins His second baptism. Do you see how all these things connect back to what John was saying in 1 John 5?

The water and the blood prove that Jesus was God's Son and He came to earth to save sinners. He was our propitiation! His blood was payment for our sin. Jesus' blood pleads before the Father to save us. We must confess that we believe in Him, and then He confesses He knows us before God, the Father. End your day in prayer telling Jesus how thankful you are that He is your Advocate.

A.C.T.S. PRAYER TIME

"Therefore everyone who confesses Me before men, I will also confess him before My Father who is in heaven." Matthew 10:32, New American Standard Bible

A (Adoration)

"Dear Lord, You are..._____"

C (Confession)

"I am sorry for..._____"

T (Thanksgiving)

"Thank You for..._____"

S (Supplication)

"Please help me..._____"

DIGGING DEEPER!

Today we studied that Jesus' blood was our propitiation for sin. Below are a few extra passages about the blood of Christ. Write what you learn on the lines.

Romans 3:23-25 _____

_____

Hebrews 2:17 _____

_____

Hebrews 9:13-15 _____

_____

1 Peter 1:18-20 _____

_____

1 John 4:10 _____

_____

DAY FIVE
ON MY KNEES:

Ta Da! You have finished another a week of Bible study. Jump down off your chair today and bow on your knees to pray to the Lord.

PRAY

"Truth. You are truth. Lord, I want to be able to tell the difference between what is true and false. Help me remember Your words so when I come across sin, I will know when to flee. I want to walk in the light. In Jesus' name, I pray. Amen."

WRITE

Open, or let your Bible voluntarily open to 1 John. Turn to Chapter 5 and write verses 11 through 13. (Remember to mark all references to God with the special symbols.)

READ

Stand up. Walk to a nearby bright spot. Read 1 John 5 aloud.

INVESTIGATIVE STUDY
STREETVIEW: CHAPTER 5

Apply!

John keeps mentioning liars. A lie is when someone doesn't tell the truth. When someone is known as a liar, you cannot trust them. God never lies so we know we can always trust Him. John wants to warn us about people who do not tell the truth. Let's look at his examples in 1 John.

Find the verses below in your Bible and circle the words "lie" or "liars" in black. If you see the word "truth," circle it in yellow. You should find eight verses with an example of liars or lying. The verses are listed on the next page, put a checkmark next to each one as you do them.

1 John 1:6	1 John 2:22
1 John 1:8	1 John 2:27
1 John 1:10	1 John 4:20
1 John 2:4	1 John 5:10

The Bible has lots to say about liars and lying. It also has lots to say about truth. We have given you a few examples. Look up the passages and write what you learn on the lines.

Psalm 101:7 _____

Psalm 119:160* _____

Proverbs 14:5 _____

John 8:31-32 _____

John 8:44 _____

A.C.T.S. Prayer Time

"Behold, I was brought forth in iniquity, and in sin my mother conceived me. Behold, You desire truth in the innermost being, and in the hidden part You will make me know wisdom. Purify me with hyssop, and I shall be clean; wash me, and I shall be whiter than snow." Psalm 51:5-7 New American Standard Bible

A (Adoration)
"Dear Lord, You are..._____"

C (Confession)
"I am sorry for..._____"

T (Thanksgiving)
"Thank You for..._____"

S (Supplication)
"Please help me..._____"

Martin Luther: Table Talk (continued)

*A continuation of last week's interview of Dr. Martin Luther with
Shelby Kennedy Foundation representatives, Anne and Grace.*

Anne: Here we are again, dining with Dr. Luther and getting his insights on some of the theological issues of his day.

Luther: You young ladies are always welcome to share our table—and join our Table Talk.

Grace: The last time we spoke with you, Dr. Luther, you mentioned "corrupt practices of the Church" as something you spoke out against. What did you mean?

Luther: I feared the Church had grown far too interested in building her reputation—and her bank account—and not interested enough in building God's reputation or adding souls to His kingdom account.

Anne: What could a Church do that would be so wrong?

Luther: Plenty. The leaders of the Church were selling what they called "indulgences." They said these slips of paper would free a soul from a place they called purgatory, an imaginary place between life and death. A person would have to buy many of these expensive indulgences in order to buy anyone's way into heaven.

Grace: Now, that's just weird.

Luther: Exactly. And not only that, it was wrong, too. Scripture clearly states that salvation comes by faith alone. So my 95 Theses argued against the use of the indulgences and other evils.

Anne: And the Church wasn't happy with those arguments, correct?

Luther: "Not happy" understates the truth. Because of the invention of the printing press, copies my 95 Theses traveled throughout Germany within two weeks and throughout Europe within a month.

Grace: So I'm guessing the Church was even more unhappy then?

Luther: Yes, indeed. Liars want nothing to do with the truth. In October, 1518, they asked me to recant—to deny what I had stated in the 95 Theses. I refused to do it unless Scripture proved me wrong.

Anne: And of course, it did not.

Luther: Of course. Later that year, I made it known to the people that the Bible did not give the pope (head of the Church) the exclusive right to interpret Scripture. People could read the Bible for themselves.

Grace: Ooh, I bet that made the pope angry.

Luther: Oh, yes. In 1520, he sent a letter that threatened to excommunicate me, or throw me out of the Church. I burned it.

Anne: Wow, you have no problem standing for the truth, do you?

Luther: None whatsoever. And the pope stood his ground, too. Not long after that, the church excommunicated me. They also banned my writings through a statement called the Edict of Worms. They said no one should read them because I was a heretic, or enemy of the faith.

Grace: Did that stop people from reading your work, Dr. Luther?

Luther: It had the opposite effect. In fact, now I had the freedom—and the platform, or ready audience—waiting to hear what I had to say.

Grace: And what did you have to say, Dr. Luther?

Luther: I'm honored you would ask. First, I had something important to do. I translated the New Testament into German so ordinary people could have the opportunity to read God's Word.

Anne: You mean they couldn't do that before?

Luther: Oh, no. My New Testament was published in 1522. Before that, the Scriptures were all in Latin, and only priests could read them. In this way, the Church kept a tight control on her people, because few knew what the Bible really said. I wanted them to be able to explore God's Word for themselves.

Grace: That sounds like a great idea to me.

Luther: Thank you. I had some more great ideas, too. I wrote hymns for the church like "A Mighty Fortress Is Our God" that explored the great truths of the faith. I started my own church, the first in what became the Lutheran denomination. In 1525, I married my dear Katharina von Bora, a former nun. Together we committed to live a life of obedience to God's Word. And in 1532, the Old Testament—which I had also translated into German, the language of the people—was published.

Anne: So it sounds like you keep busy with ministry and with your marriage.

Luther: Very much so. Katharina and I had six children together, three boys and three girls. I continue to teach in the university setting and through my home, where we have boarded and mentored more than a thousand students through the years. Some of my assistants—Philip Melanchthon, for example—have gone on to be important theologians in their own right.

Grace: So if you were going to sum up your life for us, how would you do it, sir?

Luther: I would have to say two things: "Here I stand" (my statement at the Diet of Worms, when I refused to recant the 95 Theses) and "Peace if possible. Truth at all costs." You cannot have real faith without truth. And I am grateful to the God who showed me the way out of darkness and into truth and light.

Anne: Grace and I are grateful for all you have done to bring truth to the world, Dr. Luther. Thank you for sharing your Table Talk with us.

DAY ONE

ON MY KNEES:

Our God is in control of everything, and promises to be our protection. We can ask Him for help any time of the day or night. Let's pray before we begin our study.

PRAY

"Lord, I am so comforted to know that You are my protection. When I call upon You, You hear my voice. May my prayers be like a pleasant aroma before You. You are my refuge. Use Your words today to strengthen me." (Psalm 141)

WRITE

Please write 1 John 5:14 and 15.

READ

Snuggle up with one of your parents and ask them to read 1 John 5 to you. After they have read, give them a hug and word of encouragement before you start your Bible study.

INVESTIGATIVE STUDY
UNDER THE RUG: WORD STUDY - "BELIEVE"

Apply!

Did you already pick some Key Words from 1 John 5? The two words that we have chosen for Chapter 5 were picked for their importance to John's letter, not how many times he used them. We will begin with the word **believe** and finish our word studies with the word **understanding**.

Can you find another instance of **believe** in 1 John 5, but in the form of faith (pistis)? Put a blue box around the word.

Now, read through the word study of the word **believe**.

PART A: If you were to look up the word **believe** in Strong's Concordance, you would find that the Strong's numbers assigned to it in 1 John are 4100 and 4102. Below are the way the words is written in English, the pronunciation, and the basic definition from the Strong's dictionary.

4100. Believe. pistuō. *pist-yoo-o;* from 1402: to have faith in, to entrust, to put trust in.

4102. Believe. pistis. *pis-tis;* from 3982: faith, conviction, reliance upon Christ for salvation; assurance

PART B: If you look up the numbers 4100 and 4102 in another Greek lexicon, you can discover further explanations of the meanings of **believe** in Greek as seen here:

4100. Believe, verb; to be persuaded, to trust, convinced, self-surrendering fellowship, fully assured and unswerving confidence.

4102. Believe, translated **Faith**, noun; to win over, persuade in truth.

PART C: Armed with your new knowledge of **pisteuo**, look up the four passages that contain the word **believe**. Circle the word in the verse in your Bible. Write who was convinced and what they were convinced of according to each verse.

1 John 5:1

Who: _____

Convinced of: _____

1 John 5:5

Who: _____

Convinced of: _____

1 John 5:10

Who: _____

Convinced of: _____

1 John 5:13

Who: _____

Convinced of: _____

Can you find another instance of **believe**, but in the noun form of **pistis**, in 1 John 5? Put a box around the word both in your Bible and your handwritten copy.

Before closing your time in prayer, skim through your handwritten copy of 1 John looking for the words **believe** and **faith**. Mark each one with a special symbol of your choosing.

A.C.T.S. Prayer Time

"Thy mercy, O Lord, is in the heavens; and thy faithfulness reacheth unto the clouds. Thy righteousness is like the great mountains; thy judgments are a great deep: O Lord, thou preservest man and beast." Psalm 36:5-6 King James Version

A (Adoration)
"Dear Lord, You are..._____ "

C (Confession)
"I am sorry for..._____ "

T (Thanksgiving)
"Thank You for..._____ "

S (Supplication)
"Please help me..._____ "

DAY TWO

ON MY KNEES:

PRAY

"Lord, sometimes the people in my life frustrate me. I need Your insight and patience. I need to react, respond and reach out in ways that honor You, and treat Your people in a right manner. Help me learn how to do this better. Amen."

WRITE

Neatly write 1 John 5:16-17 on the next lines of your "Write" pages.

READ

Grab a friend and take turns reading three or four verses of 1 John 5 until you have read the whole chapter. Pray for one another and then carry on individually with your study.

INVESTIGATIVE STUDY
UNDER THE RUG: CROSS REFERENCES - "BELIEVE"

Are you ready? Are you learning your way around the books of the Bible? Today, we will travel through the Bible seeking more information about the word **believe**. Watch how **believe** and **faith** go hand in hand. Let's go!

Find and read Mark 1:14-15.

What was Jesus preaching? _____

What did He tell the people to **believe**? _____

Find and read John 3:36.

Who does a person have to **believe** in to have eternal/everlasting life?

_____

What two things happen to the person who does not **believe** in Jesus?

_____   _____

Find and read Acts 10:38-43*.

Whose life story is being told in this passage? _____

What does the person who **believes** in Jesus receive, according to verse 43?

_____

     In 1 Peter 2:6, we hear that those who **believe** in Jesus will not be disappointed. Jesus is our hope, our way, truth and life! Go to your prayer time proclaiming the praises of Jesus. He saved you from the darkness and brings you into His marvelous light!

Apply!

     Gather some or your siblings and/or friends to play a game of "Sword Drill" (races to find Bible passages). Divide into two teams. Ask a parent to use the passages with the word believe from today and yesterday's INVESTIGATIVE STUDY for the first races. Make sure to read each verse out loud. After you have used up all the believe passages, begin at Week One of your Sword Study and do more drills. Or, you could have an older sibling find new passages with the word believe or faith.

A.C.T.S. Prayer Time

"Blessed are those whose lawless deeds have been forgiven, and whose sins have been covered. Blessed is the man whose sin the Lord will not take into account."
Romans 4:7-8 New American Standard Bible

A (Adoration)
"Dear Lord, You are..._____"

C (Confession)
"I am sorry for..._____"

T (Thanksgiving)
"Thank You for..._____"

S (Supplication)
"Please help me..._____"

DAY THREE

ON MY KNEES:

Have you ever won a prize? Have you earned an award? Doing well takes practice and work. Learning what God wants works the same way. If we want to walk in the light, we have to study the Word of God to know how the Lord wants us to live. Let's pray before we continue to learn how to walk well!

PRAY

"How kind of You, Lord, to give me the Bible as my Handbook to success. Thank You for providing Your Word so that I do not have to guess what is good. Open my mind to understand Your words today."

WRITE

Turn to your "My Copy of 1 John" and write 1 John 5:18-19.

READ

Before you begin your Greek word study, please read Chapter 5 of 1 John.

INVESTIGATIVE STUDY
UNDER THE RUG: WORD STUDY -
"UNDERSTANDING"

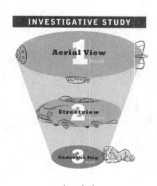

Apply!

Isn't it great when a light bulb goes off and you suddenly understand something? Isn't it a bummer when it takes forever to understand something?

The Word of God says that our hearts are deceitful and that we are not to lean on our own *understanding*. Let's look at the Greek word study of *understanding* and see what we learn about the *understanding* that John spoke of in 1 John 5.

<u>PART A:</u> If you were to look up the word *understanding* in Strong's Concordance, you would find that the Strong's number assigned to it in 1 John 5:20 is 1271. Below are the ways the words are written in English, the pronunciation,

and the basic definition from the Strong's dictionary.

1271. *Understanding.* <u>dianoia</u>. *dee-an-oy-yah; from 1223 and 3563: deep thought of the mind.*

PART B: If you look up the number in another Greek dictionary, you can discover further explanations of the meaning of **understanding** in Greek as seen here:

1. A thinking through, mature thought; activity of thinking with the heart.

The word **understanding** is only found one time in 1 John 5. Can you find it? Write the reference here:

_____

This verse is very important. Answer all of the questions on this ONE verse.

Where did the Son of God come? _____

What did He give us? _____

What word is repeated three times? _____

Who is the Son of God? _____

Why did the Son of God come? _____

Jesus coming gives us **understanding** so that we can know the truth about God, the Father. Jesus gives us **understanding** in our hearts that His Father is true and gives us eternal life! Tomorrow, we will look at more verses to that tell us what we can **understand** because of Jesus.

A.C.T.S. Prayer Time

"Trust in the Lord with all thine heart; and lean not unto thine own understanding. In all thy ways acknowledge him, and he shall direct thy paths."

Proverbs 3:5-6 King James Version

A (Adoration)

"Dear Lord, You are..._____"

C (Confession)

"I am sorry for..._____"

T (Thanksgiving)

"Thank You for..._____"

S (Supplication)

"Please help me..._____"

DAY FOUR

ON MY KNEES:

Jesus knows that you are young in years, but He says not to let anyone look down on you because you are young. He knows you can do *big things* for Him. Just keep growing in His wisdom. Go to Him in prayer.

PRAY

"Jesus, You are my Good Shepherd. I want to dwell in Your Word. Show me more understanding through my investigation of Your words to me. In Jesus' name, I pray."

WRITE

Today is noteworthy! You will finish your copy of 1 John today as you write verses 20 and 21 of 1 John 5. Well done!

READ

Re-read 1 John 5 before completing your Day 10 Diagram.

INVESTIGATIVE STUDY
UNDER THE RUG: CROSS REFERENCES – "UNDERSTANDING"

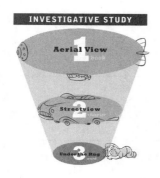

Apply!

Cross References for Understanding

Let's play a little game with our cross references for **understanding**. On the left side are passages that tell you something about the word **understanding**. On the right side are sentences that summarize each of the passages. Draw a line to match the passage reference with the summary sentence. Have fun in the Word!

(Some translators used the word *mind* or *heart* instead of *understanding*.)

Matthew 22:36-40*	We should trust in the Lord, not what we understand.
Ephesians 1:18	
	You should buy wisdom and understanding!
Psalm 119:169	
	Paul prayed that we would understand the greatness of our inheritance!
Proverbs 3:5-6	
Proverbs 23:23	Cry to the Lord for understanding.
	Jesus said that we are to love God with every bit of our understanding.

Would you say that you have a better understanding of 1 John than you did eleven weeks ago?! Oh, the blessings that the Lord gives to His diligent student! Return to your knees in prayer as you close Chapter 5.

A.C.T.S. Prayer Time

"Let my cry come before You, O Lord; give me understanding according to Your word."
Psalm 119:169 English Standard Version

A (Adoration)

"_____"

C (Confession)

"_____"

T (Thanksgiving)

"_____"

S (Supplication)

"_____"

DAY FIVE
ON MY KNEES:

Wahoo! You have come before the Lord 55 times to study 1 John. How wonderful! Today, you will complete your last Day 10 Diagram. Before you begin your summary activity, go before the Lord in prayer.

PRAY

"Lord, help me to slow down today. Put Your lessons in my memory forever so I don't forget all I have learned in 1 John. I want to bravely live for You. Amen."

WRITE

Take a few minutes to review Chapter 5. Are there any references to God? Mark them with your symbols.

READ

Read 1 John 5 using your own handwritten copy. Try not to get delayed by any of your own notes!

1-2-3 SUMMARIZE! – CHAPTER 5

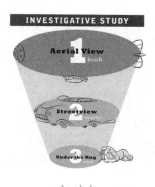

Apply!

Amazing! After you complete this final Diagram, you will have a five page, pictorial summary of the book of 1 John. Quickly, look back at the first four Diagrams to see how they lead up to this final Diagram.

☐ To begin, look at the top of the Day 10 Diagram. Fill in the chapter number. Look at Week 1, Day 5 for the original title you created for 1 John 5. Review what you wrote and refine your title with the new insights that you have learned over the last 10 days.

☐ Next, which verse from the chapter do you think was the "key verse?"

☐ On the right of the page, transfer your key Greek words from this chapter. Write the English words on the top line after the words "Greek Words." Transfer the Greek spellings and write a short definition of their meanings.

☐ On the bottom of the Diagram page, transfer the most important things that you learned about God through marking the references about Him on your "Write!" pages.

Let's join our young fellow Believers as they conclude their journey through 1 John. Since John finishes his letter in Chapter 5 with a fervent defense of the gospel, we find them in the courtroom where the message (testimony) that God has given us eternal life in His Son, Jesus Christ, is on trial. (Hint: see verses 7-8)

Right now, John is introducing the list of witnesses that testify that Jesus is the Son of God. On the chart behind John, write in each witness that he mentions in Chapter 5.

The young Believers know that they can rejoice in the outcome of this hearing, because they **believe** John's encouragement that "he who is in them is greater than he that is in the world." Write the word, "Victor" on each of their pennants, and note any three of John's descriptions of the Children of God from Chapter 5 on the blanks to the right of the Believers. There are quite a few in this chapter, pick your favorites!

Though darkness glowers on the opposite side of the courtroom, the scales make it clear whose testimony holds the greater weight of truth; label each side of the scales with the two kinds of testimony that John names in verse 5:9.

In the climax of the trial, the cross of Christ gloriously prevails on the witness stand. No argument can cloud its reassuring proclamation of 1 John 5:13; in the shining starburst above the cross, write the exhortation, "**Believe**!" On the paper nailed to the cross, write what we can be sure of when we believe in the name of the Son of God. Conclude by filling in the final lines on the witness stand with the two words that describe Who we can know, Who we dwell in, and Who Christ is, according to verse 5:20. The case is closed, the verdict is undeniable: as believers in Jesus Christ, we can rejoice, secure in the knowledge that we will live forever with God!

A.C.T.S. Prayer Time

"But as many as received Him, to them He gave the right to become children of God, to those who believe in His name: who were born, not of blood, nor of the will of the flesh, nor of the will of man, but of God." John 1:12-13 New King James Version

A (Adoration)
"Dear Lord, You are..._____"

C (Confession)
"I am sorry for..._____"

T (Thanksgiving)
"Thank You for..._____"

S (Supplication)
"Please help me..._____"

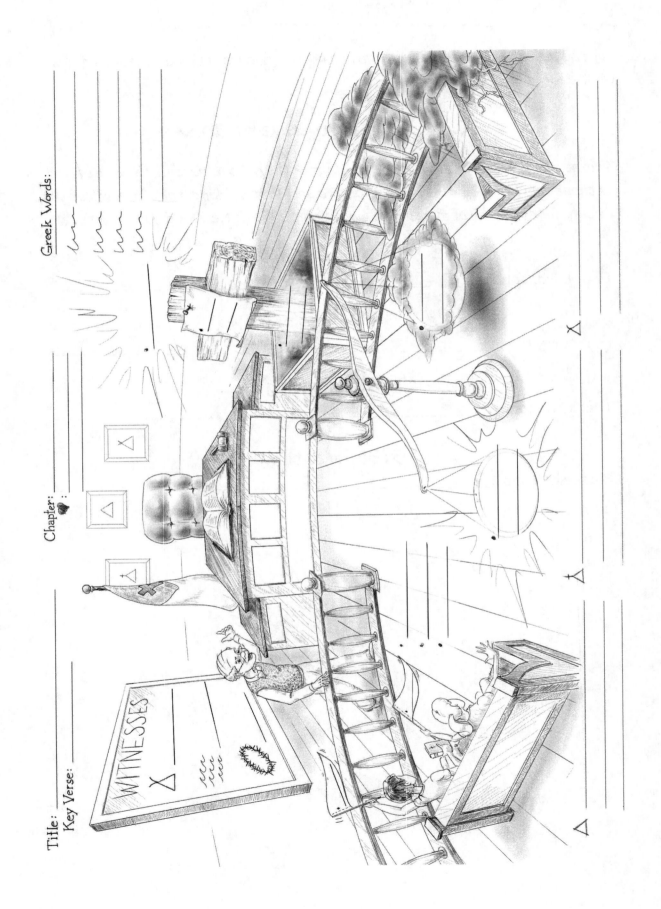

Title: _____

Key Verse: _____

Chapter: _____

Greek Words: _____

216

The Return

Andrew, Karissa and Melanie walked back into the church building after telling the last of the other families good-bye. The Local Bible Bee Contest and Celebration had ended only an hour or so before.

"Can you believe how cute those little Primaries were saying their verses?" Karissa said. "I'm so glad Dad let us help with the younger children!"

"Hey, I'm still in the Primary division," Melanie protested. "And I'm not little."

"No, you're not," encouraged Andrew. "Only one more year, and you get to move up. Did you hear us cheering?"

"Oh, yes," Melanie smiled. "And Mom gave me lots of jobs, too. I liked holding Mrs. Jamieson's baby best. He's sooo cute!"

"I know!" Karissa agreed. "I loved seeing people we hadn't seen since last year's Bee. And so many new ones, too."

"And they've become our friends because of the summer Bible Bee events," Andrew added. "Without the Bee, I never would have gotten to know Nelson, Ben, and Jesse."

"You know, I think you're talking about fellowship," Mom added as she and Dad joined the three children. "Just like we learned about in our Sword Study."

"That's right," Andrew said, "and thanks for everything you guys did so that we could be a part of this- I know putting the Bee together was lots of work."

Dad smiled. "Yes, and we are tired. But whenever I think about all those families digging deeper into God's Word, I know it's worth it."

Just then, Mom's cell phone rang. A smile brightened her face as she saw the name that lit up her screen. "It's your grandma. I'll take the call in the sanctuary. That way, your dad and I can double-check on the cleaning," she said. "Can you find something to do?"

"Sure, Mom," Karissa answered. "No problem." Turning to her brother and sister, she suggested, "Why don't we do the same thing out here? Let's make sure it's ready for church tomorrow. We don't want them to have anything left to do."

"Sounds good," Andrew agreed. Opening a closet, he told his sisters, "Maybe I can find a—"

"Broom?" said the apostle John, stepping out of the closet and handing Andrew the needed tool.

"Wow," said Andrew and Karissa together.

"Hi!" said Melanie. "You like to show up when Mom leaves, don't you?"

"You've got me figured out," John laughed as he shook out his robe. "That closet might be fine for cleaning supplies, but it's a tight fit for me."

"We don't need encouragement this time," said Melanie. "We already did this year's Sword Study!"

"I know." John grinned. "But I want to hear what you learned."

"Did you miss the Bible Bee?" Melanie asked.

"I did," John answered. "But I'm not talking about the contest."

"What's Dad been telling us?" Andrew put in as he swept up a small dust pile. "The purpose of the Sword Study is the same as the purpose of 1 John. And that's ..."

"To know the truth" his sisters finished.

"That's right!" John's smile lit up the room. "Can you tell me more?"

"Fellowship," Melanie offered. "God wants us to have fellowship one with another."

"Fellowship," John mused. "Like this room? A place to eat?"

"Of course not," Melanie was grinning now. "Fellowship means partnership, true sharing. We only have real fellowship with those who know God. And we come to know God by believing in Jesus and obeying His commandments."

"You've got it!" said John.

"God also wants us to have fellowship with Him." Karissa added. "He wants us to draw near to Him through His Word. And He wants us to spend time with Him."

"You've got it, too," John affirmed.

"Excuse me, but what I've got is an idea," Andrew was sponging down the stainless steel counters. "Let's see if Dad and Mom will stop at the Shake Shoppe on the way home."

"The Shake Shoppe," John mused. "An ice cream place?"

"Yeah!" Excitement filled Melanie's voice. "My favorite!"

"But Mel," Andrew looked into his youngest sister's eyes. "This time, Dad and Mom aren't going to treat us. This time, *we'll* get them any kind of ice cream *they* want."

"Oh," Melanie gave him a big smile. "Like, 'Love one another, because love comes from God'?"

"Exactly," the others said in unison.

"I could get used to loving people that way," said Melanie. "The ice cream way!"

"Kids," Mom's voice sounded from down the hall. John vanished as suddenly as he had appeared.

The three children grinned at each other and walked over to meet their mother.

"Hey, Mom," Andrew said. "We've got an idea."

"Your dad and I have an idea, too," Mom said. "Dad thinks because you three worked so hard on your Sword Studies and helped me so much with the Local Bee, it's time for a special treat."

"A special treat?" Melanie asked. "Ice cream?"

"Something even sweeter," Mom said. "We don't know yet if any of you qualified for the National Bible Bee Competition. But no matter what, we've decided to take a trip to go to Nationals this fall. We'll make it a family vacation!"

"Yay!" "Awesome!" "I can't believe it!" the three children shouted. "When do we go?"

"It happens about mid-November," Mom said. "We'll look at the calendar. I think we can volunteer at the Bee and still take some day trips in the area. The hotel even has a water park!"

"That sounds great! And so does stopping at The Shake Shoppe on the way home," Andrew continued. "Our treat."

"Yes," Melanie added. "Because we want to have fellowship. And love one another—the ice cream way."

DAY ONE

ON MY KNEES:

You did it! You have arrived at the last week of your 1 John Sword Study! This week, we are going to review one chapter of 1 John every day.

PRAY

"Thank You, Jesus, for teaching me so much about 1 John. Help me to continue to seek You every day and begin the study of another book of Your Word very soon. Praise You for Your gift of salvation and friendship! In Jesus' name, amen."

WRITE

God is the light. You know His light. You are one of His lights! Enjoy writing Matthew 5:16* as a reminder of what you should do as a child of God. If you have memorized it, write out the passage and then check it!

_____

_____

_____

_____

_____

READ
Open back to 1 John, Chapter 1 and read the chapter.

INVESTIGATIVE STUDY
DAY 10 DIAGRAM #1: 1 JOHN CHAPTER 1

INVESTIGATIVE STUDY

Aerial View **1**

Streetview **2**

Under the Rug **3**

Apply!

REVIEW

Fill in the blank Day 10 Diagram on the next page by memory or by looking at Chapter 1 in your Bible. Afterward, look back at your Day 10 Diagram from Week 3, Day 5 for 1 John.

A.C.T.S. PRAYER TIME

"The Lord opens the eyes of the blind; The Lord raises up those who are bowed down; The Lord loves the righteous; The Lord protects the strangers; He supports the fatherless and the widow, But He thwarts the way of the wicked."
Psalm 146:8-9 New American Standard Bible

A (Adoration)
"Dear Lord, You are..._____"

C (Confession)
"I am sorry for..._____"

T (Thanksgiving)
"Thank You for..._____"

S (Supplication)
"Please help me..._____"

Title:

Key Verse:

Chapter: ___ : ___

Greek Words:

DAY TWO

ON MY KNEES:

PRAY

WRITE

Write Proverbs 28:13-14* in the lines below. This passage is a good cross reference to Chapter 2.   If you have memorized it, write out the passage and then check it!

_____

_____

_____

_____

_____

READ
Turn in your Bible to 1 John, Chapter 2 and read the chapter.

INVESTIGATIVE STUDY
DAY 10 DIAGRAM #2: 1 JOHN CHAPTER 2

REVIEW

Apply!

Fill in the blank Day 10 Diagram on the next page by memory or by looking at Chapter 2 in your Bible. Afterward, look back at your Day 10 Diagram from Week 5, Day 5 for 1 John.

A.C.T.S. PRAYER TIME

"For the Lord God is a sun and shield; The Lord will give grace and glory; No good thing will He withhold From those who walk uprightly."
Psalm 84:11 New King James Version

A (Adoration)
"Dear Lord, You are..._____"

C (Confession)
"I am sorry for..._____"

T (Thanksgiving)
"Thank You for..._____"

S (Supplication)
"Please help me..._____"

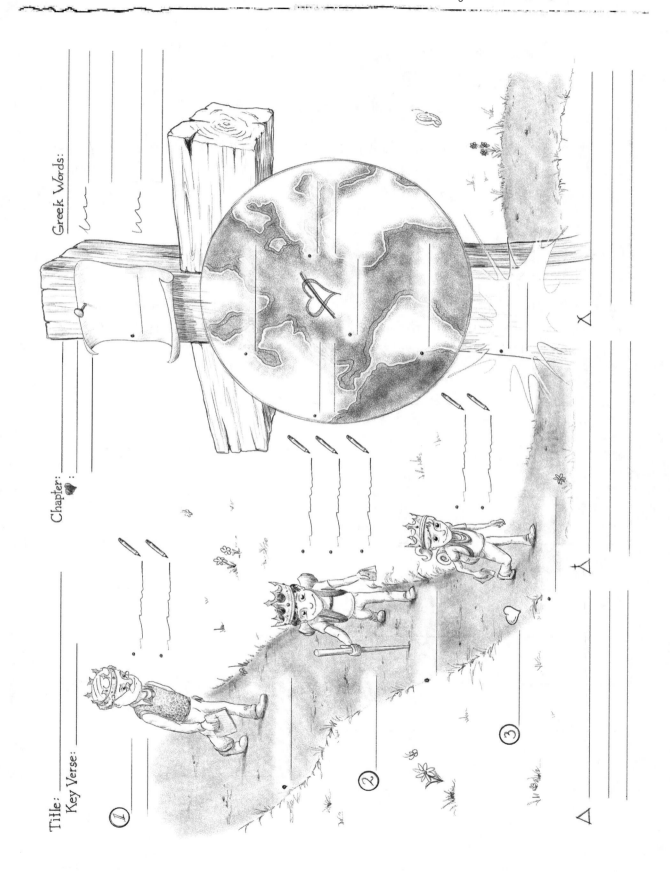

Greek Words:

Chapter:

Title:
Key Verse:

DAY THREE

ON MY KNEES:

Before we return to the review process, go before the Lord in prayer to ask for His additional insights and memories of what we have learned from John in the third chapter of 1 John.

PRAY

WRITE

Write Hosea 6:3-6* on the lines below. As we draw near to the completion of our study of 1 John, this Hosea passage is such a great reminder to press on in our pursuit of knowing the Lord. We encourage you to begin thinking about what you will study next in God's Word, as soon as you finish this week.

_____

_____

_____

_____

_____

_____

_____

_____

READ
Read Chapter 3 of 1 John before your chapter review.

INVESTIGATIVE STUDY
DAY 10 DIAGRAM #3: 1 JOHN CHAPTER 3

REVIEW
Fill in the blank Day 10 Diagram on the next page by memory or by looking at Chapter 3 in your Bible. Afterward, look back at your Day 10 Diagram from Week 7, Day 5 for 1 John.

Apply!

A.C.T.S. PRAYER TIME

"And the Scripture was fulfilled which saith, Abraham believed God, and it was imputed unto him for righteousness: and he was called the Friend of God." James 2:23 KJV

A (Adoration)
"Dear Lord, You are..._____"

C (Confession)
"I am sorry for..._____"

T (Thanksgiving)
"Thank You for..._____"

S (Supplication)
"Please help me..._____"

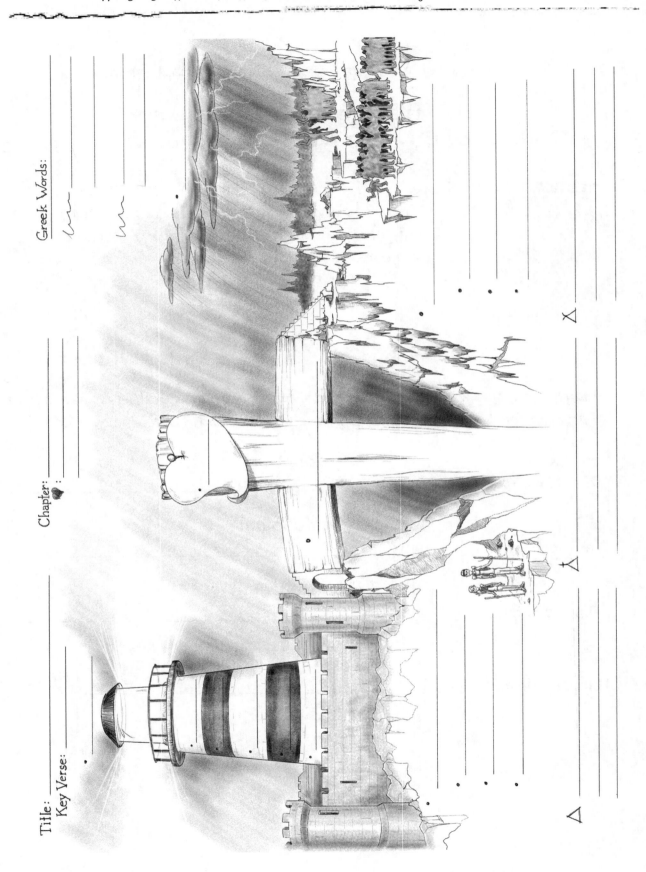

Title:

Key Verse:

Chapter: :

Greek Words:

DAY FOUR

ON MY KNEES:

Before we return to the review process, go before the Lord in prayer to ask for His additional insights and memories of what we have learned from John in the fourth chapter of 1 John.

PRAY

WRITE

Write 1 John 5:13 in the lines below. Remember, child of God, you have eternal life with Jesus. If you have memorized it, write out the passage and then check it!

_____

_____

_____

_____

_____

READ

1 John, Chapter 4 is your reading assignment for today.

Investigative Study
Day 10 Diagram #4: 1 John Chapter 4

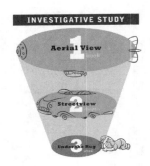

Apply!

REVIEW

Fill in the blank Day 10 Diagram on the next page by memory or by looking at Chapter 4 in your Bible. Afterward, look back at your Day 10 Diagram from Week 9, Day 5 for 1 John.

A.C.T.S. Prayer Time

"Jesus said unto him, Thou shalt love the Lord thy God with all thy heart, and with all thy soul, and with all thy mind. This is the first and great commandment."
Matthew 22:37-3 King James Version

A (Adoration)
"Dear Lord, You are..._____"

C (Confession)
"I am sorry for..._____"

T (Thanksgiving)
"Thank You for..._____"

S (Supplication)
"Please help me..._____"

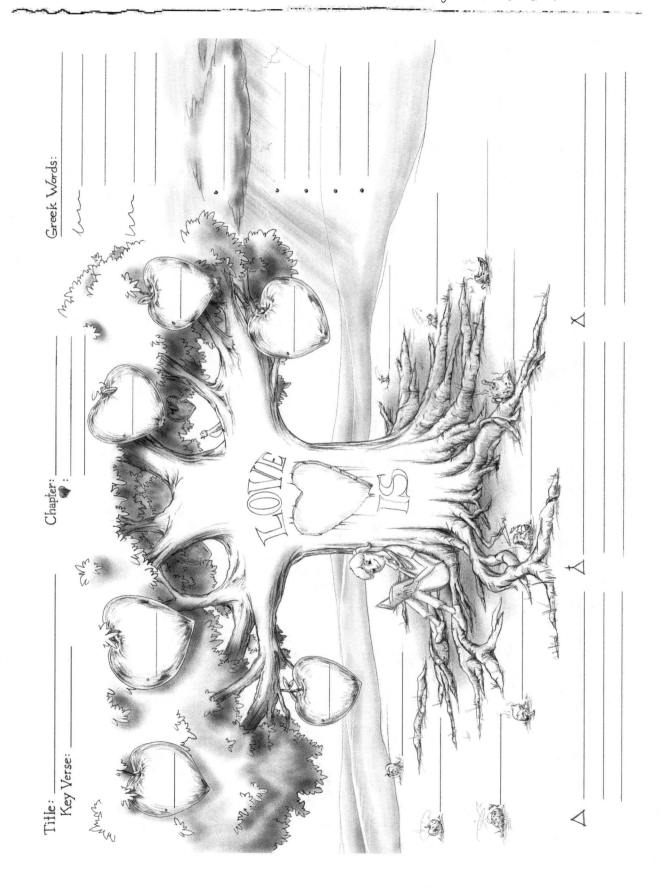

Greek Words:

Chapter: : :

Title:
Key Verse:

DAY FIVE

ON MY KNEES:

The Lord has given you new insights. He is the Light! You have fellowshipped with Him and accomplished great things by finishing your investigative study of 1 John! Praise the Lord in prayer as you begin your final day of your Sword Study of 1 John!

PRAY

WRITE

Finish your Bible study as you began it 11 weeks ago by writing Jeremiah 9:23-24* on the lines below. If you have memorized it, write out the passage and then check it!

_____

_____

_____

_____

_____

_____

_____

READ
Can you guess what we are going to ask you to do? Yes! Please read John's letter from start to finish.

INVESTIGATIVE STUDY

DAY 10 DIAGRAM #5: 1 JOHN CHAPTER 5

Apply!

REVIEW

Fill in the blank Day 10 Diagram on the next page by memory or by looking at Chapter 5 in your Bible. Afterward, look back at your Day 10 Diagram from Week 11, Day 5 for 1 John.

A.C.T.S. PRAYER TIME

"The fear of the LORD is the beginning of wisdom; A good understanding have all those who do His commandments; His praise endures forever."
Psalm 111:10 NASB

A (Adoration)
"Dear Lord, You are..._____"

C (Confession)
"I am sorry for..._____"

T (Thanksgiving)
"Thank You for..._____"

S (Supplication)
"Please help me..._____"

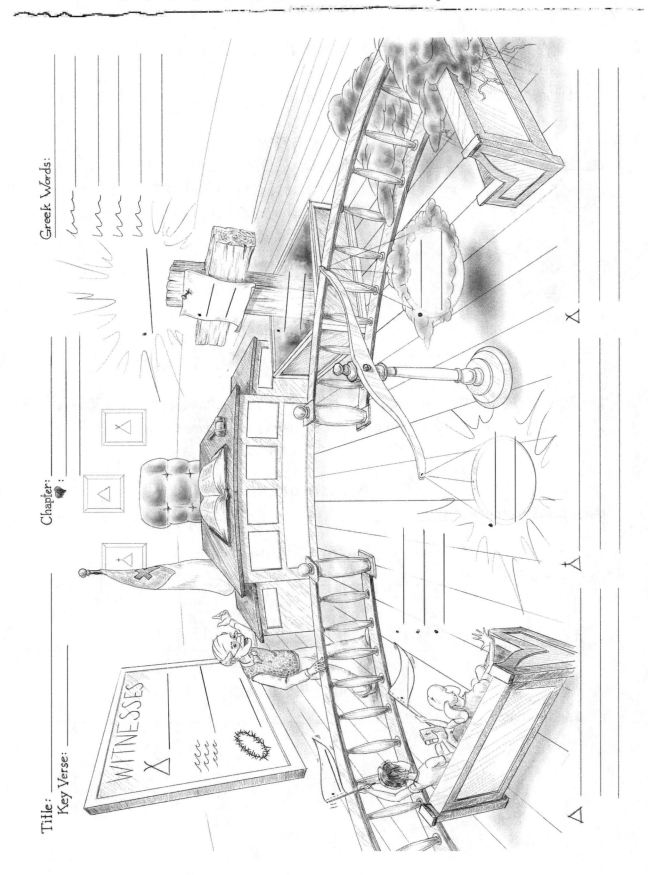

Congratulations!

You are at the finish line of this race! Well done!

Many times in life the end of one thing is the beginning of another.
We hope that will be true here. You have finished this study of 1 John,
but we hope that you will never finish studying the Bible.
The end of this study can be the beginning of the adventure of studying your
Bible for the rest of your life!
Our prayer for you is that you would …

"Have trusted Jesus for a salvation.
Love the Lord deeply with all your heart.
Love others.
Walk in obedience.
Know your God.
Be confident in your eternal life.
Fellowship daily with the Father, Son and His people.
May the peace of Christ be with you until we meet."

What book will you pick next?

WRITE!
MY COPY OF 1 JOHN

English	Greek Word	Further Definitions	Page
Fellowship	koinonia	partnership, communion & fellow travelers	

GOD
the Father

GOD
the Son

GOD
the Holy Spirit

GOD
the Father

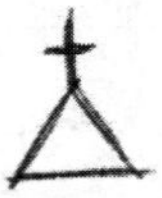

GOD
the Son

GOD
the Holy Spirit

GOD
the Father

GOD
the Son

GOD
the Holy Spirit

GOD
__the Father__

GOD
__the Son__

GOD
__the Holy Spirit__

GOD
the Father

GOD
the Son

GOD
the Holy Spirit

GOD
the Father

GOD
the Son

GOD
the Holy Spirit

GOD
the Father

GOD
the Son

GOD
the Holy Spirit

GOD
the Father

GOD
the Son

GOD
the Holy Spirit

MY COPY OF 1 JOHN 5

GOD
the Father

GOD
the Son

GOD
the Holy Spirit

GOD
the Father

GOD
the Son

GOD
the Holy Spirit

2 Timothy

Become fellow learners together with Timothy under Paul's tutelage as you learn, day by day, to be unashamed workmen who are thoroughly equipped in the everlasting truth of Scripture. This 10-week, age-leveled inductive study is perfect for one person or the whole family to do together.

Available at your Christian Bookstore

I Peter*

Discover how the lessons for first-century persecuted Christians apply to your life today. This 12-week, age-leveled inductive study is geared for a longer daily study and includes Day 10 Diagrams, a prayer journal and much more!

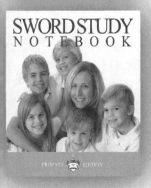

Colossians*

This original Sword Study will reveal how Christ is our all in all, as you step through 12 weeks of systematic exploration of Paul's letter to the church at Colossae. Daily study is supplemented by a prayer journal and Bible Memory passages.

*Available only online at Store.BibleBee.org

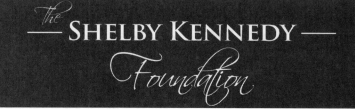

SHELBY KENNEDY
Foundation

Did you enjoy this study?

We Still Deliver!

There are three ways to continue your growth...

1. **If you have children ages 7-18, join us next Summer for The National Bible Bee.**

   - All materials delivered to you on June 1st.
   - Same inductive study method.
   - Same whole-family synchronized materials.
   - New Bible book to study each summer.
   - Meet like-minded families near you.
   - Win great prizes, with over $260,000 awarded at Nationals.

   Answer all your questions at www.BibleBee.org

2. **If you just want the next study as soon as it is available, order it directly from The Shelby Kennedy Foundation at Store.BibleBee.org**

3. **Buy one of our other Sword Study titles at your local Christian bookstore.**

www.SwordStudy.org | (937) 382-7250
www.BibleBee.org

ESV

John 8:12

12 Again Jesus spoke to them, saying, "I am the light of the world. Whoever follows me will not walk in darkness, but will have the light of life."

John 8:12

Week 2   ESV

1 John 1:3

3 that which we have seen and heard we proclaim also to you, so that you too may have fellowship with us; and indeed our fellowship is with the Father and with his Son Jesus Christ.

1 John 1:3

Week 3   ESV

Job 15:14-16

14 What is man, that he can be pure? Or he who is born of a woman, that he can be righteous? 15 Behold, God puts no trust in his holy ones, and the heavens are not pure in his sight; 16 how much less one who is abominable and corrupt, a man who drinks injustice like water!

Job 15:14-16

Week 4   ESV

Psalm 36:7-10

7 How precious is your steadfast love, O God! The children of mankind take refuge in the shadow of your wings.
8 They feast on the abundance of your house, and you give them drink from the river of your delights. 9 For with you is the fountain of life; in your light do we see light. 10 Oh, continue your steadfast love to those who know you, and your righteousness to the upright of heart!

Psalm 36:7-10

Week 5   ESV

Isaiah 43:1-2

1 But now thus says the LORD, he who created you, O Jacob, he who formed you, O Israel: "Fear not, for I have redeemed you; I have called you by name, you are mine.
2 When you pass through the waters, I will be with you; and through the rivers, they shall not overwhelm you; when you walk through fire you shall not be burned, and the flame shall not consume you.

Isaiah 43:1-2

Week 6   ESV

John 17:3

3 And this is eternal life, that they know you the only true God, and Jesus Christ whom you have sent.

John 17:3

Week 2   ESV

Proverbs 28:13-14

13 Whoever conceals his transgressions will not prosper, but he who confesses and forsakes them will obtain mercy. 14 Blessed is the one who fears the LORD always, but whoever hardens his heart will fall into calamity.

Proverbs 28:13-14

Week 4   ESV

1 John 1:9

9 If we confess our sins, he is faithful and just to forgive us our sins and to cleanse us from all unrighteousness.

1 John 1:9

Week 3   ESV

2 Corinthians 6:16-18

16 What agreement has the temple of God with idols? For we are the temple of the living God; as God said, "I will make my dwelling among them and walk among them, and I will be their God, and they shall be my people. 17 Therefore go out from their midst, and be separate from them, says the Lord, and touch no unclean thing; then I will welcome you, 18 and I will be a father to you, and you shall be sons and daughters to me, says the Lord Almighty."

2 Corinthians 6:16-18

Week 6   ESV

John 8:31-32

31 So Jesus said to the Jews who had believed him, "If you abide in my word, you are truly my disciples, 32 and you will know the truth, and the truth will set you free."

John 8:31-32

Week 5   ESV

ESV

Isaiah 45:22-23

22 "Turn to me and be saved, all the ends of the earth! For I am God, and there is no other. 23 By myself I have sworn; from my mouth has gone out in righteousness a word that shall not return: 'To me every knee shall bow, every tongue shall swear allegiance.'

Isaiah 45:22-23

Week 7   ESV

Philippians 3:8-11

8 Indeed, I count everything as loss because of the surpassing worth of knowing Christ Jesus my Lord. For his sake I have suffered the loss of all things and count them as rubbish, in order that I may gain Christ 9 and be found in him, not having a righteousness of my own that comes from the law, but that which comes through faith in Christ, the righteousness from God that depends on faith— 10 that I may know him and the power of his resurrection, and may share his sufferings, becoming like him in his death, 11 that by any means possible I may attain the resurrection from the dead.

Philippians 3:8-11

Week 8   ESV

2 Corinthians 5:14-15

14 For the love of Christ controls us, because we have concluded this: that one has died for all, therefore all have died; 15 and he died for all, that those who live might no longer live for themselves but for him who for their sake died and was raised.

2 Corinthians 5:14-15

Week 9   ESV

Psalm 119:160

160 The sum of your word is truth, and every one of your righteous rules endures forever.

Psalm 119:160

Week 10   ESV

Matthew 22:36-40

36 "Teacher, which is the great commandment in the Law?" 37 And he said to him, "You shall love the Lord your God with all your heart and with all your soul and with all your mind. 38 This is the great and first commandment. 39 And a second is like it: You shall love your neighbor as yourself. 40 On these two commandments depend all the Law and the Prophets."

Matthew 22:36-40

Week 11   ESV

Hosea 6:3-6

3 Let us know; let us press on to know the LORD; his going out is sure as the dawn; he will come to us as the showers, as the spring rains that water the earth." 4 What shall I do with you, O Ephraim? What shall I do with you, O Judah? Your love is like a morning cloud, like the dew that goes early away. 5 Therefore I have hewn them by the prophets; I have slain them by the words of my mouth, and my judgment goes forth as the light. 6 For I desire steadfast love and not sacrifice, the knowledge of God rather than burnt offerings.

Hosea 6:3-6

Week 12   ESV

1 John 4:7-10

7 Beloved, let us love one another, for love is from God, and whoever loves has been born of God and knows God. 8 Anyone who does not love does not know God, because God is love. 9 In this the love of God was made manifest among us, that God sent his only Son into the world, so that we might live through him. 10 In this is love, not that we have loved God but that he loved us and sent his Son to be the propitiation for our sins.

1 John 4:7-10

Week 8 ESV

2 Corinthians 5:20-21

20 Therefore, we are ambassadors for Christ, God making his appeal through us. We implore you on behalf of Christ, be reconciled to God. 21 For our sake he made him to be sin who knew no sin, so that in him we might become the righteousness of God.

2 Corinthians 5:20-21

Week 7 ESV

1 John 5:13

13 I write these things to you who believe in the name of the Son of God that you may know that you have eternal life.

1 John 5:13

Week 10 ESV

Ephesians 5:1-4

1 Therefore be imitators of God, as beloved children. 2 And walk in love, as Christ loved us and gave himself up for us, a fragrant offering and sacrifice to God. 3 But sexual immorality and all impurity or covetousness must not even be named among you, as is proper among saints. 4 Let there be no filthiness nor foolish talk nor crude joking, which are out of place, but instead let there be thanksgiving.

Ephesians 5:1-4

Week 9 ESV

Matthew 5:14-16

14 "You are the light of the world. A city set on a hill cannot be hidden. 15 Nor do people light a lamp and put it under a basket, but on a stand, and it gives light to all in the house. 16 In the same way, let your light shine before others, so that they may see your good works and give glory to your Father who is in heaven.

Matthew 5:14-16

Week 12 ESV

Acts 10:38-43

38 how God anointed Jesus of Nazareth with the Holy Spirit and with power. He went about doing good and healing all who were oppressed by the devil, for God was with him. 39 And we are witnesses of all that he did both in the country of the Jews and in Jerusalem. They put him to death by hanging him on a tree, 40 but God raised him on the third day and made him to appear, 41 not to all the people but to us who had been chosen by God as witnesses, who ate and drank with him after he rose from the dead. 42 And he commanded us to preach to the people and to testify that he is the one appointed by God to be judge of the living and the dead. 43 To him all the prophets bear witness that everyone who believes in him receives forgiveness of sins through his name."

Acts 10:38-43

Week 11 ESV

Psalm 111:10

10 The fear of the LORD is the beginning of wisdom: a good understanding have all they that do his commandments: his praise endureth for ever.

Psalm 111:10

Week 1   KJV

John 8:12

12 Then spake Jesus again unto them, saying, I am the light of the world: he that followeth me shall not walk in darkness, but shall have the light of life.

John 8:12

Week 2   KJV

1 John 1:3

3 That which we have seen and heard declare we unto you, that ye also may have fellowship with us: and truly our fellowship is with the Father, and with his Son Jesus Christ.

1 John 1:3

Week 3   KJV

Job 15:14-16

14 What is man, that he should be clean? and he which is born of a woman, that he should be righteous? 15 Behold, he putteth no trust in his saints; yea, the heavens are not clean in his sight. 16 How much more abominable and filthy is man, which drinketh iniquity like water?

Job 15:14-16

Week 4   KJV

Psalm 36:7-10

7 How excellent is thy lovingkindness, O God! therefore the children of men put their trust under the shadow of thy wings. 8 They shall be abundantly satisfied with the fatness of thy house; and thou shalt make them drink of the river of thy pleasures. 9 For with thee is the fountain of life: in thy light shall we see light. 10 O continue thy lovingkindness unto them that know thee; and thy righteousness to the upright in heart.

Psalm 36:7-10

Week 5   KJV

Isaiah 43:1-2

1 But now thus saith the LORD that created thee, O Jacob, and he that formed thee, O Israel, Fear not: for I have redeemed thee, I have called thee by thy name; thou art mine. 2 When thou passest through the waters, I will be with thee; and through the rivers, they shall not overflow thee: when thou walkest through the fire, thou shalt not be burned; neither shall the flame kindle upon thee.

Isaiah 43:1-2

Week 6   KJV

John 17:3

3 And this is life eternal, that they might know thee the only true God, and Jesus Christ, whom thou hast sent.

John 17:3

Week 2   KJV

Jeremiah 9:23-24

23 Thus saith the LORD, Let not the wise man glory in his wisdom, neither let the mighty man glory in his might, let not the rich man glory in his riches: 24 But let him that glorieth glory in this, that he understandeth and knoweth me, that I am the LORD which exercise lovingkindness, judgment, and righteousness, in the earth: for in these things I delight, saith the LORD.

Jeremiah 9:23-24

Week 1   KJV

Proverbs 28:13-14

13 He that covereth his sins shall not prosper: but whoso confesseth and forsaketh them shall have mercy. 14 Happy is the man that feareth always: but he that hardeneth his heart shall fall into mischief.

Proverbs 28:13-14

Week 4   KJV

1 John 1:9

9 If we confess our sins, he is faithful and just to forgive us our sins, and to cleanse us from all unrighteousness.

1 John 1:9

Week 3   KJV

2 Corinthians 6:16-18

16 And what agreement hath the temple of God with idols? for ye are the temple of the living God; as God hath said, I will dwell in them, and walk in them; and I will be their God, and they shall be my people. 17 Wherefore come out from among them, and be ye separate, saith the Lord, and touch not the unclean thing; and I will receive you, 18 And will be a Father unto you, and ye shall be my sons and daughters, saith the Lord Almighty.

2 Corinthians 6:16-18

Week 6   KJV

John 8:31-32

31 Then said Jesus to those Jews which believed on him, If ye continue in my word, then are ye my disciples indeed; 32 And ye shall know the truth, and the truth shall make you free.

John 8:31-32

Week 5   KJV

Isaiah 45:22-23

22 Look unto me, and be ye saved, all the ends of the earth: for I am God, and there is none else. 23 I have sworn by myself, the word is gone out of my mouth in righteousness, and shall not return, That unto me every knee shall bow, every tongue shall swear.

Isaiah 45:22-23

Week 7 KJV

Philippians 3:8-11

8 Yea doubtless, and I count all things but loss for the excellency of the knowledge of Christ Jesus my Lord: for whom I have suffered the loss of all things, and do count them but dung, that I may win Christ, 9 And be found in him, not having mine own righteousness, which is of the law, but that which is through the faith of Christ, the righteousness which is of God by faith: 10 That I may know him, and the power of his resurrection, and the fellowship of his sufferings, being made conformable unto his death; 11 If by any means I might attain unto the resurrection of the dead.

Philippians 3:8-11

Week 8   KJV

2 Corinthians 5:14-15

14 For the love of Christ constraineth us; because we thus judge, that if one died for all, then were all dead: 15 And that he died for all, that they which live should not henceforth live unto themselves, but unto him which died for them, and rose again.

2 Corinthians 5:14-15

Week 9   KJV

Psalm 119:160

160 Thy word is true from the beginning: and every one of thy righteous judgments endureth for ever.

Psalm 119:160

Week 10   KJV

Matthew 22:36-40

36 Master, which is the great commandment in the law? 37 Jesus said unto him, Thou shalt love the Lord thy God with all thy heart, and with all thy soul, and with all thy mind. 38 This is the first and great commandment. 39 And the second is like unto it, Thou shalt love thy neighbour as thyself. 40 On these two commandments hang all the law and the prophets.

Matthew 22:36-40

Week 11   KJV

Hosea 6:3-6

3 Then shall we know, if we follow on to know the LORD: his going forth is prepared as the morning; and he shall come unto us as the rain, as the latter and former rain unto the earth. 4 O Ephraim, what shall I do unto thee? O Judah, what shall I do unto thee? for your goodness is as a morning cloud, and as the early dew it goeth away. 5 Therefore have I hewed them by the prophets; I have slain them by the words of my mouth: and thy judgments are as the light that goeth forth. 6 For I desired mercy, and not sacrifice; and the knowledge of God more than burnt offerings.

Hosea 6:3-6

Week 12   KJV

1 John 4:7-10

7 Beloved, let us love one another: for love is of God; and every one that loveth is born of God, and knoweth God. 8 He that loveth not knoweth not God; for God is love. 9 In this was manifested the Love of God toward us, because that God sent his only begotten Son into the world, that we might live through him. 10 Herein is Love, not that we loved God, but that he loved us, and sent his Son To be the propitiation for our sins.

1 John 4:7-10

Week 8 KJV

2 Corinthians 5:20-21

20 Now then we are ambassadors for Christ, as though God did beseech you by us: we pray you in Christ's stead, be ye reconciled to God. 21 For he hath made him to be sin for us, who knew no sin; that we might be made the righteousness of God in him.

2 Corinthians 5:20-21

Week 7   KJV

1 John 5:13

13 These things have I written unto you that believe on the name of the Son of God; that ye may know that ye have eternal life, and that ye may believe on the name of the Son of God.

1 John 5:13

Week 10 KJV

Ephesians 5:1-4

1 Be ye therefore followers of God, as dear children; 2 And walk in love, as Christ also hath loved us, and hath given himself for us an offering and a sacrifice to God for a sweetsmelling savour. 3 But fornication, and all uncleanness, or covetousness, let it not be once named among you, as becometh saints; 4 Neither filthiness, nor foolish talking, nor jesting, which are not convenient: but rather giving of thanks.

Ephesians 5:1-4

Week 9 KJV

Matthew 5:14-16

14 Ye are the light of the world. A city that is set on an hill cannot be hid. 15 Neither do men light a candle, and put it under a bushel, but on a candlestick; and it giveth light unto all that are in the house. 16 Let your light so shine before men, that they may see your good works, and glorify your Father which is in heaven.

Matthew 5:14-16

Week 12 KJV

Acts 10:38-43

38 How God anointed Jesus of Nazareth with the Holy Ghost and with power: who went about doing good, and healing all that were oppressed of the devil; for God was with him. 39 And we are witnesses of all things which he did both in the land of the Jews, and in Jerusalem; whom they slew and hanged on a tree: 40 Him God raised up the third day, and showed him openly; 41 Not to all the people, but unto witnesses chosen before of God, even to us, who did eat and drink with him after he rose from the dead. 42 And he commanded us to preach unto the people, and to testify that it is he which was ordained of God to be the Judge of quick and dead. 43 To him give all the prophets witness, that through his name whosoever believeth in him shall receive remission of sins.

Acts 10:38-43

Week 11 KJV

Psalm 111:10

10 The fear of the LORD is the beginning of wisdom; A good understanding have all those who do His commandments; His praise endures forever.

Psalm 111:10

Week 1   NASB

John 8:12

12 Then Jesus again spoke to them, saying, " I am the Light of the world; he who follows Me will not walk in the darkness, but will have the Light of life."

John 8:12

Week 2   NASB

1 John 1:3

3 what we have seen and heard we proclaim to you also, so that you too may have fellowship with us; and indeed our fellowship is with the Father, and with His Son Jesus Christ.

1 John 1:3

Week 3   NASB

Job 15:14-16

14 "What is man, that he should be pure, Or he who is born of a woman, that he should be righteous? 15 "Behold, He puts no trust in His holy ones, And the heavens are not pure in His sight; 16 How much less one who is detestable and corrupt, Man, who drinks iniquity like water!

Job 15:14-16

Week 4   NASB

Psalm 36:7-10

7 How precious is Your lovingkindness, O God! And the children of men take refuge in the shadow of Your wings. 8 They drink their fill of the abundance of Your house; And You give them to drink of the river of Your delights. 9 For with You is the fountain of life; In Your light we see light. 10 O continue Your lovingkindness to those who know You, And Your righteousness to the upright in heart.

Psalm 36:7-10

Week 5   NASB

Isaiah 43:1-2

1 But now, thus says the LORD, your Creator, O Jacob, And He who formed you, O Israel, "Do not fear, for I have redeemed you; I have called you by name; you are Mine! 2 "When you pass through the waters, I will be with you; And through the rivers, they will not overflow you. When you walk through the fire, you will not be scorched, Nor will the flame burn you.

Isaiah 43:1-2

Week 6   NASB

John 17:3

3 "This is eternal life, that they may know You, the only true God, and Jesus Christ whom You have sent.

John 17:3

Week 2   NASB

Jeremiah 9:23-24

3 Thus says the LORD, " Let not a wise man boast of his wisdom, and let not the mighty man boast of his might, let not a rich man boast of his riches; 24 but let him who boasts boast of this, that he understands and knows Me, that I am the LORD who exercises lovingkindness, justice and righteousness on earth; for I delight in these things," declares the LORD.

Jeremiah 9:23-24

Week 1   NASB

Proverbs 28:13-14

3 He who conceals his transgressions will not prosper, But he who confesses and forsakes them will find compassion. 14 How blessed is the man who fears always, But he who hardens his heart will fall into calamity.

Proverbs 28:13-14

Week 4   NASB

1 John 1:9

9 If we confess our sins, He is faithful and righteous to forgive us our sins and to cleanse us from all unrighteousness.

1 John 1:9

Week 3   NASB

2 Corinthians 6:16-18

16 Or what agreement has the temple of God with idols? For we are the temple of the living God; just as God said, " I WILL DWELL IN THEM AND WALK AMONG THEM; AND I WILL BE THEIR GOD, AND THEY SHALL BE MY PEOPLE. 17 " Therefore, COME OUT FROM THEIR MIDST AND BE SEPARATE," says the Lord. "AND DO NOT TOUCH WHAT IS UNCLEAN; And I will welcome you. 18 " And I will be a father to you, And you shall be sons and daughters to Me," Says the Lord Almighty.

2 Corinthians 6:16-18

Week 6   NASB

John 8:31-32

31 So Jesus was saying to those Jews who had believed Him, " If you continue in My word, then you are truly disciples of Mine; 32 and you will know the truth, and the truth will make you free."

John 8:31-32

Week 5   NASB

NASB

Isaiah 45:22-23

22 " Turn to Me and be saved, all the ends of the earth; For I am God, and there is no other. 23 " I have sworn by Myself, The word has gone forth from My mouth in righteousness And will not turn back, That to Me every knee will bow, every tongue will swear allegiance.

Isaiah 45:22-23

Week 7 NASB

Philippians 3:8-11

8 More than that, I count all things to be loss in view of the surpassing value of knowing Christ Jesus my Lord, for whom I have suffered the loss of all things, and count them but rubbish so that I may gain Christ, 9 and may be found in Him, not having a righteousness of my own derived from the Law, but that which is through faith in Christ, the righteousness which comes from God on the basis of faith, 10 that I may know Him and the power of His resurrection and the fellowship of His sufferings, being conformed to His death; 11 in order that I may attain to the resurrection from the dead.

Philippians 3:8-11

Week 8   NASB

2 Corinthians 5:14-15

14 For the love of Christ controls us, having concluded this, that one died for all, therefore all died; 15 and He died for all, so that they who live might no longer live for themselves, but for Him who died and rose again on their behalf.

2 Corinthians 5:14-15

Week 9   NASB

Psalm 119:160

160 The sum of Your word is truth, And every one of Your righteous ordinances is everlasting.

Psalm 119:160

Week 10   NASB

Matthew 22:36-40

36 "Teacher, which is the great commandment in the Law?" 37 And He said to him, " ' YOU SHALL LOVE THE LORD YOUR GOD WITH ALL YOUR HEART, AND WITH ALL YOUR SOUL, AND WITH ALL YOUR MIND.' 38 "This is the great and foremost commandment. 39 "The second is like it, 'YOU SHALL LOVE YOUR NEIGHBOR AS YOURSELF.' 40 "On these two commandments depend the whole Law and the Prophets."

Matthew 22:36-40

Week 11 NASB

Hosea 6:3-6

3 "So let us know, let us press on to know the LORD. His going forth is as certain as the dawn; And He will come to us like the rain, Like the spring rain watering the earth." 4 What shall I do with you, O Ephraim? What shall I do with you, O Judah? For your loyalty is like a morning cloud And like the dew which goes away early. 5 Therefore I have hewn them in pieces by the prophets; I have slain them by the words of My mouth; And the judgments on you are like the light that goes forth. 6 For I delight in loyalty rather than sacrifice, And in the knowledge of God rather than burnt offerings.

Hosea 6:3-6

Week 12 NASB

1 John 4:7-10

7 Beloved, let us love one another, for love is from God; and everyone who loves is born of God and knows God. 8 The one who does not love does not know God, for God is love. 9 By this the love of God was manifested in us, that God has sent His only begotten Son into the world so that we might live through Him. 10 In this is love, not that we loved God, but that He loved us and sent His Son to be the propitiation for our sins.

1 John 4:7-10

Week 8 NASB

2 Corinthians 5:20-21

20 Therefore, we are ambassadors for Christ, as though God were making an appeal through us; we beg you on behalf of Christ, be reconciled to God. 21 He made Him who knew no sin to be sin on our behalf, so that we might become the righteousness of God in Him.

2 Corinthians 5:20-21

Week 7 NASB

1 John 5:13

13 These things I have written to you who believe in the name of the Son of God, so that you may know that you have eternal life.

1 John 5:13

Week 10 NASB

Ephesians 5:1-4

1 Therefore be imitators of God, as beloved children; 2 and walk in love, just as Christ also loved you and gave Himself up for us, an offering and a sacrifice to God as a fragrant aroma. 3 But immorality or any impurity or greed must not even be named among you, as is proper among saints; 4 and there must be no filthiness and silly talk, or coarse jesting, which are not fitting, but rather giving of thanks.

Ephesians 5:1-4

Week 9 NASB

Matthew 5:14-16

14 "You are the light of the world. A city set on a hill cannot be hidden; 15 nor does anyone light a lamp and put it under a basket, but on the lampstand, and it gives light to all who are in the house. 16 "Let your light shine before men in such a way that they may see your good works, and glorify your Father who is in heaven.

Matthew 5:14-16

Week 12 NASB

Acts 10:38-43

38 "You know of Jesus of Nazareth, how God anointed Him with the Holy Spirit and with power, and how He went about doing good and healing all who were oppressed by the devil, for God was with Him. 39 "We are witnesses of all the things He did both in the land of the Jews and in Jerusalem. They also put Him to death by hanging Him on a cross. 40 "God raised Him up on the third day and granted that He become visible, 41 not to all the people, but to witnesses who were chosen beforehand by God, that is, to us who ate and drank with Him after He arose from the dead. 42 "And He ordered us to preach to the people, and solemnly to testify that this is the One who has been appointed by God as Judge of the living and the dead. 43 Of Him all the prophets bear witness that through His name everyone who believes in Him receives forgiveness of sins."

Acts 10:38-43

Week 11 NASB

The SHELBY KENNEDY Foundation

Psalm 111:10

10 The fear of the LORD is the beginning of wisdom; A good understanding have all those who do His commandments. His praise endures forever.

Psalm 111:10

Week 1 NKJV

John 8:12

12 Then Jesus spoke to them again, saying, "I am the light of the world. He who follows Me shall not walk in darkness, but have the light of life."

John 8:12

Week 2 NKJV

1 John 1:3

3 that which we have seen and heard we declare to you, that you also may have fellowship with us; and truly our fellowship is with the Father and with His Son Jesus Christ.

1 John 1:3

Week 3 NKJV

Job 15:14-16

14 "What is man, that he could be pure? And he who is born of a woman, that he could be righteous? 15 If God puts no trust in His saints, And the heavens are not pure in His sight, 16 How much less man, who is abominable and filthy, Who drinks iniquity like water!

Job 15:14-16

Week 4 NKJV

Psalm 36:7-10

7 How precious is Your lovingkindness, O God! Therefore the children of men put their trust under the shadow of Your wings. 8 They are abundantly satisfied with the fullness of Your house, And You give them drink from the river of Your pleasures. 9 For with You is the fountain of life; In Your light we see light. 10 Oh, continue Your lovingkindness to those who know You, And Your righteousness to the upright in heart.

Psalm 36:7-10

Week 5 NKJV

Isaiah 43:1-2

1 But now, thus says the LORD, who created you, O Jacob, And He who formed you, O Israel: "Fear not, for I have redeemed you; I have called you by your name; You are Mine. 2 When you pass through the waters, I will be with you; And through the rivers, they shall not overflow you. When you walk through the fire, you shall not be burned, Nor shall the flame scorch you.

Isaiah 43:1-2

Week 6 NKJV

NKJV

John 17:3

3 And this is eternal life, that they may know You, the only true God, and Jesus Christ whom You have sent.

John 17:3

Week 2   NKJV

Jeremiah 9:23-24

23 Thus says the LORD: "Let not the wise man glory in his wisdom, Let not the mighty man glory in his might, Nor let the rich man glory in his riches; 24 But let him who glories glory in this, That he understands and knows Me, That I am the LORD, exercising lovingkindness, judgment, and righteousness in the earth. For in these I delight," says the LORD.

Jeremiah 9:23-24

Week 1   NKJV

Proverbs 28:13-14

13 He who covers his sins will not prosper, But whoever confesses and forsakes them will have mercy. 14 Happy is the man who is always reverent, But he who hardens his heart will fall into calamity.

Proverbs 28:13-14

Week 4   NKJV

1 John 1:9

9 If we confess our sins, He is faithful and just to forgive us our sins and to cleanse us from all unrighteousness.

1 John 1:9

Week 3   NKJV

2 Corinthians 6:16-18

16 And what agreement has the temple of God with idols? For you are the temple of the living God. As God has said: "I will dwell in them And walk among them. I will be their God, And they shall be My people." 17 Therefore "Come out from among them And be separate, says the Lord. Do not touch what is unclean, And I will receive you." 18 "I will be a Father to you, And you shall be My sons and daughters, Says the LORD Almighty."

2 Corinthians 6:16-18

Week 6   NKJV

John 8:31-32

31 Then Jesus said to those Jews who believed Him, "If you abide in My word, you are My disciples indeed. 32 And you shall know the truth, and the truth shall make you free."

John 8:31-32

Week 5   NKJV

NKJV

Isaiah 45:22-23

22 "Look to Me, and be saved, All you ends of the earth! For I am God, and there is no other. 23 I have sworn by Myself; The word has gone out of My mouth in righteousness, And shall not return, That to Me every knee shall bow, Every tongue shall take an oath.

Isaiah 45:22-23

Week 7   NKJV

Philippians 3:8-11

8 Yet indeed I also count all things loss for the excellence of the knowledge of Christ Jesus my Lord, for whom I have suffered the loss of all things, and count them as rubbish, that I may gain Christ 9 and be found in Him, not having my own righteousness, which is from the law, but that which is through faith in Christ, the righteousness which is from God by faith; 10 that I may know Him and the power of His resurrection, and the fellowship of His sufferings, being conformed to His death, 11 if, by any means, I may attain to the resurrection from the dead.

Philippians 3:8-11

Week 8   NKJV

2 Corinthians 5:14-15

14 For the love of Christ compels us, because we judge thus: that if One died for all, then all died; 15 and He died for all, that those who live should live no longer for themselves, but for Him who died for them and rose again.

2 Corinthians 5:14-15

Week 9   NKJV

Psalm 119:160

160 The entirety of Your word is truth, And every one of Your righteous judgments endures forever.

Psalm 119:160

Week 10   NKJV

Matthew 22:36-40

36 "Teacher, which is the great commandment in the law?" 37 Jesus said to him, ""You shall love the LORD your God with all your heart, with all your soul, and with all your mind.' 38 This is the first and great commandment. 39 And the second is like it: "You shall love your neighbor as yourself.' 40 On these two commandments hang all the Law and the Prophets."

Matthew 22:36-40

Week 11   NKJV

Hosea 6:3-6

3 Let us know, Let us pursue the knowledge of the LORD. His going forth is established as the morning; He will come to us like the rain, Like the latter and former rain to the earth. 4 "O Ephraim, what shall I do to you? O Judah, what shall I do to you? For your faithfulness is like a morning cloud, And like the early dew it goes away. 5 Therefore I have hewn them by the prophets, I have slain them by the words of My mouth; And your judgments are like light that goes forth. 6 For I desire mercy and not sacrifice, And the knowledge of God more than burnt offerings.

Hosea 6:3-6

Week 12   NKJV

The SHELBY KENNEDY Foundation

NKJV

1 John 4:7-10

7 Beloved, let us love one another, for love is of God; and everyone who loves is born of God and knows God. 8 He who does not love does not know God, for God is love. 9 In this the love of God was manifested toward us, that God has sent His only begotten Son into the world, that we might live through Him. 10 In this is love, not that we loved God, but that He loved us and sent His Son to be the propitiation for our sins.

1 John 4:7-10

Week 8 NKJV

2 Corinthians 5:20-21

20 Now then, we are ambassadors for Christ, as though God were pleading through us: we implore you on Christ's behalf, be reconciled to God. 21 For He made Him who knew no sin to be sin for us, that we might become the righteousness of God in Him.

2 Corinthians 5:20-21

Week 7 NKJV

1 John 5:13

13 These things I have written to you who believe in the name of the Son of God, that you may know that you have eternal life, and that you may continue to believe in the name of the Son of God.

1 John 5:13

Week 10 NKJV

Ephesians 5:1-4

1 Therefore be imitators of God as dear children. 2 And walk in love, as Christ also has loved us and given Himself for us, an offering and a sacrifice to God for a sweet-smelling aroma. 3 But fornication and all uncleanness or covetousness, let it not even be named among you, as is fitting for saints; 4 neither filthiness, nor foolish talking, nor coarse jesting, which are not fitting, but rather giving of thanks.

Ephesians 5:1-4

Week 9 NKJV

Matthew 5:14-16

14 "You are the light of the world. A city that is set on a hill cannot be hidden. 15 Nor do they light a lamp and put it under a basket, but on a lampstand, and it gives light to all who are in the house. 16 Let your light so shine before men, that they may see your good works and glorify your Father in heaven.

Matthew 5:14-16

Week 12 NKJV

Acts 10:38-43

38 how God anointed Jesus of Nazareth with the Holy Spirit and with power, who went about doing good and healing all who were oppressed by the devil, for God was with Him. 39 And we are witnesses of all things which He did both in the land of the Jews and in Jerusalem, whom they killed by hanging on a tree. 40 Him God raised up on the third day, and showed Him openly, 41 not to all the people, but to witnesses chosen before by God, even to us who ate and drank with Him after He arose from the dead. 42 And He commanded us to preach to the people, and to testify that it is He who was ordained by God to be Judge of the living and the dead. 43 To Him all the prophets witness that, through His name, whoever believes in Him will receive remission of sins.

Acts 10:38-43

Week 11 NKJV